Performance Day

Short Stories, Poems, Film Criticism, and Other Writings from a Curious Teen

AMIR ALI SAID

Brooklyn, NY

Performance Day: Short Stories, Poems, and Other Writings
from a Curious Teen
By Amir Ali Said

 Published by Superchamp Books, a Division of Superchamp, Inc. P.O. Box 20274, Brooklyn, New York 11202-0274; (347) 263-7865. www.superchampbooks.com.

Edited by Amir Said

About the Author photo by Amir Said © 2012 Amir Said
Cover, Design, and Layout by Amir Said Copyright © 2013 Amir Said

Print History:
March 2013: First printing.
September 2013: Second printing.
April 2015: Third printing.

Performance Day: Poems, Short Stories, and Other Writings
from a Curious Teen / by Amir Ali Said
1. Short Stories 2. Poetry 3. Film Criticsm 4. Youth Writers 5. Memoir
I. Title

Library of Congress Control Number: 2013934449
ISBN 978-0-9749704-4-8 (Paperback)

Pop… *As-Salaam wa-laikum, wa-Rahmatullah, wa-Barakatahu.* Pop, I could write an entire book about my gratitude and thanks to you. Thank you for teaching me how to write. Thank you for teaching me how to play basketball. Thank you for teaching me how to play baseball. Thank you for teaching me how to think. Thank you for inspiring me to write—to write anything, everyday! Thank you for encouraging me to screen films day in and day out. Thank you for all the advice and all of our discussions. Thank you for teaching me how to be a thoughtful human being. And thank you for all of the Superchamp rounds. I've learned so much from you since I entered this world. You're my hero. Finally, thank you for encouraging me to write this book. I'm grateful to Allah that you are my father… And I thank Allah for keeping you on earth every step of the way with me for all of my 16 years. May Allah bless you.

Ummee… *As-Salaam wa-laikum, wa-Rahmatullah, wa-Barakatahu.* Umee, thanks for the trips to the museums, the cupcakes and all the candy. Thank you for "Steaky, Mac, and Green." Thank you for the swimming lessons and all the field trips. Thank you for Madden! If it wasn't for you, Pop and I wouldn't have had it. Thank you for always believing in me. Thank you for your constant support, and most importantly, your love. May Allah bless you.

For my father, Amir Said.
Pop, you are my one true friend.
You are my most important gift.
Insha' Allah…Al-Humdullilah.

Acknowledgements

Laurie Spigel—I can not thank you enough. The past three years with you in your literary club have been one of the most important and rewarding experiences in my life. Thank you for your infinite knowledge of literature, film, and life as a whole. You helped inspire me to read and write more. Thank you for suggesting and giving me new books. Thank you for inviting me to improv. You have been a wonderful presence in my life.

Charissa Martin—Thank you for offering a film class! Many of the films you first brought to my attention will have a lasting impact on my career as a writer, filmmaker, and actor.

Rebecca Wallace-Segall–Thank you for starting Writopia, and creating an atmosphere that's supportive and helpful. Thank you for creating a platform where I can flush out my ideas and communicate freely with other teenage writers. Finally, I want to thank you for continuing to be a wonderful, tireless instructor and leader, and supporter of my writing.

Rita-Jo "RJ" Houston—Thank you for your Shakespeare class. Thank you for casting me in my first play, Shakespeare's *The Comedy of Errors*. Being introduced seriously to Shakespeare through you has been tremendously beneficial to me. Thank you for sharing your knowledge of the Bard and theater in general.

Ellen Gilbert, Rachel Altman, Jaime Pillet, and Bonnie Shumofsky (Abrams)—Thank you for being great agents, and finding me good film and television projects. All of my bookings have been a big help to my writing, and none of them would ever have happened without the work that you all do. Cheers!

Evelyn Polesny—Thank you for your insightful approach to literature (and life in general). I appreciate all of the books that you introduced me to; and thank you for kindness. Oh, and thank for the chocolate chip bread!

The New York City Homeschooling Community—Thank you for being a vibrant, welcoming, and nurturing community filled with a lot of bright, kind, helpful, and wonderful people. I could not have made my successful transition out of NYC Public

School system without you!

Dan Kitrosser (Writopia)—Thank you for your constant encouragement, help, and huge support.

Courtney Sheinmel (Writopia)—Thank you for always remembering I want pretzels during snack time! And thank you for all of your writing help. Writopia is fortunate to have you.

Finbarr Wilbrink—Thank you for your help with the first play I ever wrote and produced. Your advice, help, and insight was great. **Rosalie Purvis (Play)**—Rosalie thank you for directing and helping me produce my second play. And thank you for reassuring me that the story I wrote happens all the time in Europe, ha! Without you, I wouldn't have been able to reign in the actors the same way. Thanks for all your time, advice, and knowledge about theater.

Leo Lion—As a fellow young writer, you've encouraged me. Thank you. **Raheem Nugent**—Thanks for being a good friend, strong supporter, and motivator. **Scott Grindley**—Thanks for being a strong supporter and motivator as well as a good friend. And thanks for answering all of my questions about football (aka soccer)!

Seth Godin—Thank you for the wisdom you share everyday.

Stephen King—Thank you for your imagination. Thank you for writing *Carrie*, and *It*, and *Rage*, and many more. And thank you for your writing style.

Finally, I would also like to extend my respect and deep gratitude to author/poet, **Sam Greenlee**, who's *Ammunition* book (and other writings) will always mean a great deal to me.

Table of Contents

OTHER WRITINGS 163

Introduction

From the start, Amir was always interested in the story of things. When he was just 3 years old, he professed that *The Birds*—perhaps Alfred Hitchcook's most haunting thriller—was his favorite movie. Once a day, sometimes twice, he would go and get *The Birds* VHS tape from off of our movie shelf, pop it into the VCR, and watch. For the most part, he would sit silently. When I asked him on numerous occasions why he liked *The Birds* so much, he'd say, "I like how what happens is organized." And so, at 3 years old, it was clear that he had an understanding of storyline and narrative... *"I like how what happens is organized."*

This type of metaphorical speech would continue to serve as Amir's means for various seemingly unrelated descriptions. At 7 years old, he called his metallic silver crayon "ice". Everywhere we went, he described different shades of gray as shades of "ice". By 12, he was drawing parallels between a boxer's uppercut and a baseball player's bat swing. This single revelation helped him become one of the best hitters I've ever seen. In the batter's box, Amir was smart, focused. Thus, like all of his interests, I attributed his skill in baseball to his mind, and the high level of thoughtfulness he applied to anything that he chose to do.

When he announced to me (a couple weeks before his 13th birthday) that he was going to write and publish his first book when he was 16, there was no doubt in my mind that he would. So what is presented here before you is a breast of work by one of the most thoughtful, creative, and determined individuals that I've ever known, and that I've had the honor and privilege to raise as my son. A father should be so fortunate....

Right. So what are you in for with *Performance Day*? Well, in "The Perfect Shot," Chris, a young, quick-thinking photojournalist, is hot on the trail of the one photo that will land him his dream job at a big time magazine… In "Brooklyn Bridge Park," a quick glance on the train between two strangers leads to an awkward new relationship… In "Get Rid of the Kid," a troubled teen is on the run from a ruthless gangster, who runs an organization of teenage contract killers… In "The Affair of Agnes Miller," an English tutor finds happiness when she gives a student a lesson in life he never expected....

These are just the brief descriptions of the fascinating short stories that anchor *Performance Day: Short Stories, Poems, and Other Writings from a Curious Teen.* In this engaging, wonderfully written collection of short stories, poems, film reviews, editorials, mini-memoirs, and more, Amir takes you into the mind of a New York City teenager, as he combines his imagination with his deep curiosity about the world around him. Written between the ages of 13 and 16, the writings in this book represent a sharp, young mind in the midst of adloscense. From emotional realizations to new intellectual and cultural horizons, Amir shares a body of work that's forthright and illuminating. Thus, I trust that you will find *Performance Day* to be entertaining, inspiring, and rewarding.

—Amir Said, Brooklyn, NY 2012

Short Stories

Brooklyn Bridge Park

The R train creeped into the station. I got on the train and blew a sigh of relief. I took the nearest pole seat and scanned the rest of the car. I looked through my jean pockets. I felt some eyes on me. I looked up and I saw a girl staring at me. She was pulling out a stick of gum. I remembered what I was looking for. I pulled out my own pack of gum. The girl and I locked eyes and we shared a smile.

She was beautiful.

She had innocent, gorgeous, blue eyes. Her dark brown hair and blonde highlights stretched down her back. She had the lips of a woman, the smile of an actress. Before I got a chance to say anything, it was my stop. Damn.

I looked through the train window as it pulled off, and we shared another smile together. Man, I'd do anything to get a chance to talk to her.

Above ground, I looked through my pockets again and noticed my blue pen was missing. Must've fell out when I was getting up off the train. That would be only the second pen I lost in two years. I hated losing pens.

I walked down a block and then another block and I found myself in the middle of a fair. There were kids running around everywhere. I was hungry. I didn't know if I should eat now, or wait until when April and I met up later. But my stomach was growling, so I scanned the block for some food joints and found a pizzeria on 9th street and Douglass Avenue.

It was a nice brick oven spot called Luigi's. I ordered a slice and sat down. Behind me, I could feel these piercing eyes on my shoulder. I looked through the mirror on the wall. This guy was watching me. I think he worked for Luigi's because he had on a white button up, the bus boy kind. But he looked kind of young about 15 or 16, so I didn't really know what to think. I stood up to see what he would do. I cuffed my jean legs and looked to the side to see if he was still watching. He was, only now, he was approaching me.

"Yo, man, you know my sister, Lee?"

I never knew that Lee was a unisex name. I tried to laugh his question off.

"Nah, man. You got the wrong dude."

"You the asshole that keeps coming round at night."

I hate it when people make scenes in public.

"Yo, son that's not me. You got me confused." He was riled up now.

"You calling me a liar? You're telling me you *didn't* walk out of my house last week?"

"Yeah, son, that's what I'm telling you. I don't know who your sister is or who you're looking for, but it aint my problem. I'm just here getting a slice."

I felt that should've ended it, but it didn't.

"Oh, word? Let me show you something."

Before the words could even register, he swung at me, and I was in the middle of a fight. His first swing was wild, I moved out of the way. I wasn't trying to fight the guy so I just played the whole bout defensively. A straight here and a jab there kept him put. He was so angry he was hitting air and everything but me in that pizzeria. The guy was winded so he didn't even see me sizing him up.

One of the workers tried to break up the fight. I heard somebody yell, "Call the police."

I caught him in his rib cage and dropped him. Then I high stepped it out of there.

I blended in with the fair.

"Hey there." An elderly woman in her late 60s said to me.

"Hello, how are you doing?" I said.

I needed some conversation to calm me down after that episode in the pizzeria.

"I'm fine and yourself?"

She had a warm demeanor. I bet her grand kids loved her.

"I'm alright. Could be better." I smiled.

I wondered if she could tell that I'd just been in a fight.

"What's a handsome young man like you doing in the fair all alone? What, you don't have a girlfriend?"

I was wondering myself. I should've been at April's house by now.

"I'm actually not in the fair, I sorta just drifted here. I'm on my way to my girlfriend's house right now."

April wasn't my girlfriend yet, but I don't know, I guess we were in a relationship.

"Well you go and find her and have your self a nice time! It's hot out here. Make sure you get her some ice cream, you hear me!?"

"I will. I promise."

She's right. It was about 90 degrees. My phone rang; it was April.

"Well it was nice meeting you mam. Have a nice day," I said with a smile. She smiled back.

"It was nice meeting you, too Hun."

I answered my phone.

"Where are you, Kevin?" she said.

"I don't know, I'm in the middle of a fair right now."

"The fair? Why are you in the middle of the fair?"

"It looked cool. So I dipped in real fast."

"Okay, so where are you exactly?"

I had to maneuver through some of the crowd to see where I was.

"I'm on 11th Street and Washington Avenue."

She sounded surprised, "Oh okay, you're close, then. Just get over here already."

"What's wrong?" I asked.

"Nothing, just get here, please."

"Gotcha." I hung up.

I was already in the middle of the fair so I had to find a way to get to the sidewalk. As I continued to walk all you could see was a sea of kids. These kids were either eating and dropping some food, or running with their friends, playing tag or some variation. The parents were all talking with one another. The cops were on patrol, but you couldn't tell by the fun they were having themselves. One officer was shooting some hoops with a couple of kids. Another officer helped some girls out with a game of double dutch. It was a pretty decent neighborhood fair, all things told.

When I got to the sidewalk, I made a B-line to the corner store. I was thirsty. Inside, I went to the back and grabbed some water and a bag of popcorn. I gave the cashier a five-dollar bill I had stashed in my pocket, got my change, and walked out.

I walked down 10th street. The whole block was filled with the fair. There was some rock group I never heard of on stage performing, The Ogres. Pretty weird name for a rock band I thought. But I continued walking. I called April when I got to 13th Street.

"April, I'm on 13th and Adams. I'll be there soon."

"Okay. My friend and I are sitting outside on my stoop."

"Alright. Cool." I hung up.

I didn't know if April realized or not that I was procrastinating. It didn't take me a half hour to get to her house, even with a couple blocks of fair goers. I just liked her neighborhood. The beauty, the calm nature of all the people. The scenery. Everything about April's neighborhood seemed to be flawless. There were families everywhere, vendors, food, beautiful buildings and brownstones. I wanted to live here; I didn't want to just come over to April's house. But coming to see her was the only chance I got to see this neighborhood. I wanted to be here all the time. Soak up the energy, the trees, the air and the people—some of them anyway.

April didn't do much to get this life. She was born into it. Her mother was a corporate lawyer and a father was a curator at the Museum of Modern Art. That's a hell of a mix if you ask me. April loved her life. Or it at least appeared so. But she took it for granted. I know she did. She also didn't really have any life goals. She went with the flow and tried to have fun all the time. That's cool and all, but at some point, I want a girlfriend I can go to the movies with and talk about them afterwards.

I reached 14th Street and Douglass. While I waited for the light to change, I saw a flock of girls coming towards me. All the girls were laughing and talking to each other and I was just looking for the prettiest one. I couldn't find her. I mean this group of girls from afar looked like a pretty click. But when they got closer, all I saw was six ugly and badly dressed girls, each with no body to speak of. Flat asses and small breasts, the whole lot of them. What made it worse was they walked with an obnoxious arrogance, like they owned the block.

I got to 15th and Douglass in no time. But again, I was waiting for the light to change. I saw a dog, a black baby rottweiler and its owner. The baby dog was in the arms of this man. Yo, *Man's best friend* and all that jazz. But what happens when that rottweiler grows up? I don't care how "trained" a dog is, I'm not sure you want to keep a dog like that around all the time. Great watch dog, I guess.

I crossed the street. As I was walking up to the house I spit the gum I had already in my mouth and threw in a new piece. I took my phone out and put it on phone calls only. I didn't want to be disturbed unless it was important. I pulled up my pants, tied my sneakers, and pulled my shirt down a little bit.

Two houses down on April's block, there were books being sold outside on tables and in crates. Good books, too. I saw several fine copies of *Great Gatsby*. And then, I saw her.

The girl from the train. Get the fuck outta here! *She* was April's friend? I walked up to them.

"Hello ladies."

"Well how do you do, mister?" April replied.

I gave her a hug. Then a quick kiss on the cheek. Normally I would have kissed April on the lips. But I didn't want to do anything to turn off the girl from the train.

"Hey, how you doing." I said to the girl from the train.

We hugged. She smelled great and she was an even better hugger.

"I'm fine." She smiled.

"Allegra, this is Kevin. Kevin this is Allegra." April was a little late with her introducing.

"Nice to meet you." Allegra said.

"The pleasure's mine," I replied.

I guess Allegra and I had an unspoken agreement not to bring up anything about seeing each other earlier on the train. She didn't say nothing, so, shit I wasn't go to say anything. So we acted like two complete strangers. I mean, we were two complete strangers, but I felt like I knew her.

"Babe, you want to come inside?" April said.

"Oh, no doubt. It's hot out here. Let's watch a flick with the A.C. on."

It was awkward enough that Allegra looked better than April. Don't get me wrong, April was pretty. It's just, Allegra was a 10, and April was more like a solid 8 with decent sized breasts. But Allegra had the breasts, ass, *and* the pretty face! She had the smile, too. Even though April and I had been getting pretty close for months now, I would've ended it right there for Allegra.

The three of us watched *The Wedding Singer* in April's living room. I sat there wondering if the day could get any weirder. I was hoping it didn't.

April was lying down under my arm and Allegra was by herself sitting next to us, but on the far side of the couch.

She was taking in the movie and texting on her phone. I was spending most of my time trying not to kiss April, or anything else I'd normally be doing with April on the couch when no one else was around.

The Wedding Singer was good. A classic comedy in my book. I was more interested in if Allegra liked it. She seemed to. She was laughing at all the right spots. She even shed a tear at the end when Robbie (Adam Sandler) sang his "I want to grow old with you" song to Julia (Drew Barrymore).

April smiled and then kissed me when Adam Sandler said that line. I was tryna see how Allegra reacted. I didn't care for all that lovey-dovey shit at the moment. When the movie was over, the three of us made our way to the kitchen. I grabbed myself a water from the fridge. April pulled out a box of strawberry pop tarts, then her and Allegra went to town on them.

Allegra was beautiful. I spent most of my time in the kitchen staring her. I almost didn't care if April saw or not.

Before I knew it, it was 5 O'Clock. That was the time April's parents usually came home on Saturdays from dance practice with April's younger sister. April walked us out of the house.

"Baby, are you coming over tomorrow after school?" April asked. "My parents are working late and my sister will be at her piano lessons."

"Nah, I can't. I got some business to take care of with my Pops." Couldn't believe I said no to April and an empty house.

"Okay. Tuesday then?"

"Yeah I got you." We kissed, much longer than I would

have liked in front of Allegra.

"So, Allegra where you going?" April said.

"I'm going home."

"You taking the R?" I interjected.

After I said it, I realized how anxious and suspicious I must've looked.

"Yeah, I am actually."

"Cool, I'm going the same way." I recovered.

"Alright, now that we've got that settled I'm gonna head back in and wait for mom and dad." Said April.

I grabbed April by her waist, kissed her again, then she went back inside. Allegra and I walked down the steps together in a single file, made a right, and continued walking down the block.

"So how old are you?" I said to Allegra.

"16. You?"

"Same. Where you from? You got this funny walk going on." I was clowning around. Wasn't anything wrong with her walk. In fact, everything was right with her walk.

She laughed.

"My walk? What's funny about it?"

"You walk like you got 6 toes."

She laughed again. "I'm from here. But my father is from Cuba, and my mother is Puerto Rican.

"How bout you? Where are you from?"

"I'm black, American. I was born here in New York."

"Really? But your hair, you sure you're not Dominican or Jamaican or something? Where did you get this curly hair from?"

When she touched my hair I was surprised. I knew it was on now. "Nah, I'm American. Word up."

"Hmm." She replied, like she didn't believe me.

"I know you liked them pop tarts, but that wasn't a real meal. You want to get something to eat with me? I'm hungry."

"Um...OK., yes, I'd like that."

I wasn't counting on her saying yes so fast. I thought I was going to have to use some charm to convince her. But when she said yes so quickly, it almost caught me off guard.

There was a pizzeria up ahead.

"What school do you go to?" I asked.

"Bishop Kearney." She replied.

"Kearney? What's that?"

"It's an all girl's catholic school."

I always wondered what went on in an all girls' school. Not even the sexual tension, but just how girls could co-exist with one another for eight hours a day and ten months out of the year.

"You like it?"

"Eh, I don't know if "like" is the word. I mean I love my friends and all, and my classes are mostly good—I guess. But I don't know, it's alright."

It sounded like she hated school.

"Damn. It sounds like your miserable there."

"Only on Thursdays." She laughed.

I didn't get the joke, but I laughed with her anyway. We got to a stoplight, about a block away from the pizzeria, and I just stopped and looked her. She was texting on her phone, so she couldn't see me.

"How long have you and April been going out?"

The light changed.

"About four months."

"Oh, wow. When'd you guys meet?"

"A while ago, at this party." Again, I kept it short and simple.

"Oh okay, cool."

"How bout you? You single?" I asked.

"*Unfortunately.*" She replied.

She had these cute puppy dog eyes, and they looked even sadder when she said that.

"You're single? Wow…somebody must of' fucked up really bad."

She laughed.

"Yeah…My last relationship didn't work out so well."

"What happened?"

"He was a jerk. He cheated on me, and he just didn't appreciate me."

The thought of someone cheating on this beautiful, sweet, innocent-looking girl amazed me.

"A guy's got to be a complete asshole to screw a relationship up with you. I just met you and I'm already in love."

There was an awkward silence, a beat, and then an awkward laugh followed.

"Oh really?"

"Yeah, well, you know what I mean," I said, covering up my tracks.

She laughed. "Yes, I understand."

I think she was fucking with me because she knew I wouldn't respond to well to those questions. Anyway, we walked into the pizzeria laughing and smiling. This time around, I took a pit stop at Mario's pizzeria. The pizzeria wasn't as fancy as the one earlier but it would serve its purpose as a last minute spot. I ordered two slices.

"Oh, no, its okay, Kevin, I'll pay."

"Nah, keep your money. I got this."

"Aww, thank you."

She smiled her pretty smile, and walked away.

We sat down. It was 5:30 now. I took the seat furthest away from the T.V. because there was a game on. That 5:00 range for television was always weird to me. Wasn't much on cable and there certainly wasn't anything on any television networks. But there always seemed to be a futbol match on at this time. Today was no different. And it wasn't just any futbol match, but El Classico, the annual rivalry game between Barcelona and Real Madrid.

"You watch world futbol?" I said.

"Soccer you mean?" she replied.

I could've gone into a historical lesson on the creation of the word soccer and how *football* was still the name of the sport around the world, and how American football was just that. But, it wasn't the setting, and she actually seemed interested. So, I let it slide.

"Oh, so you do watch it? Who's your favorite team?" I asked.

"Definitely, Man U."

"Say word. Mine too."

"Do you play soccer yourself or you just a big fan?" she asked.

"At the moment, no. How bout you?"

"I used to play."

"What position did you play?"

"Forward, center midfielder, and sometimes right back."

"Wow, so we've got a soccer star in the building," I said.

She laughed.

I liked the vibes Allegra gave off. She wasn't cocky or arrogant, just an overall sweet, nice person.

"I used to play baseball. Some of the best years of my life. I was planning on playing in high school. But then I realized it wasn't for me, and I just quit after my last season of little league."

"Wow, you must've been really good." She said.

The thought of my baseball dream, and how the decision I made to walk away, always loomed large. I missed it sometimes.

"Yeah, you can say that."

"So what do you do now? Since you're done with sports and all."

"I'm a writer." I said.

"Oh, you write? What sort of things do you write about?" she asked.

It was an innocent inquiry. But it felt good knowing someone was interested in what you do.

"Stories, short stories, poetry, sports, anything really. I just feel like there's so much to write about and not enough time, so I try to do as much as I can."

"Wow, I've never met a boy who likes to write. I'm always stuck with a jock or something."

"I guess you get the best of both worlds with me then, right?"

She laughed.

"Ha! You could say that."

The pizza came. I forgot to get us drinks.

"What you wanna drink?"

"A sprite, please," she said politely with a smile.

"Alright, cool."

I went back to the front of the pizzeria and got us two cold canned sprites. I spent the last of my cash on those sprites. I walked back over to where we were eating and placed the sprites down.

"This is cool?" I asked.

"Yeah, but I think anything would be better than this pizza right now."

We both started laughing.

"Man, I thought I was the only one. Let's just take these sprites and go."

"Wait, the game's not over yet."

"It's 2-1. Barcelona's going to win. Watch, trust me."

"Alright, if you say so, genius." I turned to head towards the door. Allegra grabbed her small chain wallet and followed me. It was 7 o'clock.

"It's kind of cold." She said.

"Come here."

She knew what she was doing.

"Going home?" I asked.

"Yeah. I'm supposed to be home by 8 on school nights."

"Oh, alright, cool."

We walked to the train station in a comfortable silence. We didn't say much to each other besides a laugh and a comment here or there we just relaxed, and took in the moment. It was something special. The sun was starting to set, and the moon was getting ready for its shift. It was all a beautiful thing.

We got to the subway station. We swiped our metro cards and walked through the turnstiles. Allegra began to make a right and I was making a left. She was going downtown and I was going uptown.

"Oh, so I don't get the pleasure of a train ride with you tonight after all."

"Sadly." She said.

"What's your number?" I asked.

"Let me see your phone."

I gave her my phone, and she put her number into my contacts, then gave my phone back to me.

"That's what's up. I'll call you tonight," I told her.

"You better," she said in a joking but soft voice.

I looked into her eyes, and I leaned in for a kiss, but she stopped me. She shook her hand in a manner that said no.

She gave me a hug and smile.

I liked that. I mean of course I wanted the kiss, but it proved that this wouldn't be easy. Plus, I was, in fact, still in a relationship with April.

I walked up the stairs leading to the uptown R train. This station was beyond complex. Instead of simply walking up the stairs leading to the R train like on the downtown side, I had to maneuver around the G train first. When I got to the R train platform it was desolate. I saw a family of three, two Hispanic girls, and a vagrant who lay beside a train bench. I stood closest to the family.

I had time to think. This whole Allegra and April situation came out of nowhere. I had a stable relationship with April, a good girl, pretty, smart and good enough I suppose. But when I laid my eyes on Allegra everything just changed. April was now expendable. Even though we'd just met, I felt more comfortable with Allegra than any other girl I'd been with before. The train came. I entered calmly, still in my own head.

When I got home, Pop wasn't there yet. I headed straight for my room and my bed. I was beat, and I wanted to take a little nap before I called Allegra. I took my sneakers off, laid back, and crashed.

When I woke up, it was 5 o'clock, the next morning. I'd slept straight through. Outside my room, I could hear Pop getting ready. I sat up on the side of my bed, wiped my eyes, and I thought of Allegra. There's no way I would be able to talk to April the same way ever again.

On my way to take a shower, I was stopped by my father.

"Yo, you were knocked out last night!"

"I know right," I said laughing. "Pop, I didn't even mean to sleep for that long. I was just exhausted when I came home."

"I could tell. I didn't want to wake you up. You were in a deep dream when I came in."

"Ha! What happen?" I asked.

"I don't know, you were just real excited though. You said something about you didn't want to go to the carnival."

"The carnival?" I laughed. "I couldn't even begin to tell you what that was about."

We both laughed.

"How's April?" my father asked.

Just then, I realized that I hadn't called Allegra.

"April's good. But her friend Allegra's better."

"I can dig it. Just be careful how you roll with it."

"I hear you." I gave my father a pound handshake, then went back to my bedroom to check my phone. There was a missed call from a number I didn't recognize, but I figured it was Allegra. There was also a missed call from April, too.

After I showered and got dressed, I walked my father to the door.

"I should be back late this afternoon, no later than 6 or so. We'll talk more later. I left money for you when you go to class"

"Alright, cool. Thank you, Pop."

My father and I gave each other a pound, then he left and I went to my desk. I wanted to call Allegra, but I didn't know if she was up yet. Then my phone rang.

"Hello?"

"Hi, Kevin." It was Allegra, of course.

"Yo, my bad, I fell asleep and slept straight through to the next morning. I was going to try and catch you before you went to school."

"Oh, don't worry about it. Just don't let that shit happen again," she said playfully.

"Ha! No doubt, I won't...By the way, I like your morning voice."

"Oh really? So you saying my day voice is ugly?"

I laughed. "I'm not saying all that, but yeah, since you brought it up, your voice is extra fugly."

She laughed.

"I hate you!" she said.

"Damn, already?"

"I'm Just playing… Listen, I don't know what your *homeschool* schedule is like today, but I wanted to know if you could meet me today right after school?"

"Of course, what time?"

"Like 6:15? I have to be in after school study hall until then."

"That's cool," I said, then I hung up the phone and went and did some reading and work from my curriculum.

At 4:30, Allegra hit me.

"Kevin, I got out of study hall early. Can you be here by 5:30? Meet me at the pizzeria, the place we tried to eat at yesterday."

"No doubt. I'm ready to roll. I'll be there in a half-hour, tops."

"Kay...See you soon."

I wasn't really ready to roll. If I was going out, I was going to have to take another shower. I don't think I ever jumped into the shower and got dressed again so quickly before in my life. I mean I levitated into the bathroom and into my clothes.

It was hotter than usual for a spring day. It had touched 80 degrees earlier that afternoon. So I had on a polo shirt sleeve, jeans, and sneakers. I was rully ready and out the door in 20 minutes.

When I got to the corner I realized I left my stick of gum at home. So I went to the corner store and bought a new one.

"Yo, Kev!" I heard somebody scream my name as I walked into the corner store. I turned around and saw it was my man Jordan. He ran across the street as the light turned green. I gave him a pound and a bear hug.

"Yo, Kev, what up man, where you been?" he asked.

"Just chillin,' working hard, you know, the regular."

"Aw, man. I hear that. I ain't see you in a minute son."

He said.

"Word, word…It's been a while. You still playing ball?"

"Yeah, but only for my AAU team. My high school coached kicked me off the team."

"Kicked you off the team? What happened?"

"I spazzed out when my uncle died. That shit hurt man."

I could see his eyes start to water. But he was holding it back.

"What? Your uncle passed? Yo, my condolences son." I said.

"Yeah, like four months ago some white dude was drunk driving, ran a red light, and my Uncle was walking across the street with his lady, he pushed her to the side and took the impact himself."

I could see the hurt in his eyes.

"Damn son…I know your uncle was like your pops. How you holding up?" I asked.

"I'm chillin' man. You know...How you, though? Where you headed?"

"Bout to go check this girl though."

"Word, she got a friend?"

"Ha!—" I saw the bus coming a block away. "Imma put you on later, the bus about to be here. Your number still the same?"

"Yeah, son, hit me up later. We gotta get up."

"I got you."

I gave Jordan another pound and bear hug, then I ran across the street to catch the bus. The bus ride was light. I got to the pizzeria in 20 minutes like I said I would. Allegra wasn't there yet, though. I called her.

"Allegra, where you at?" I said.

I could hear the bus engine and air conditioner in the background.

"I'm on the bus. Where are you?"

"I'm here!"

She laughed.

"Aw, I'm sorry. I'll be there in a second. I'm like two stops away."

"Yeah, Alright. Make it snappy," I said.

She laughed.

"Okay, bye."

When I hung up the phone and began digging through my pockets I realize I still didn't have any gum. There wasn't a deli or corner store in sight. I walked three blocks and still couldn't find one. I looked to my left, then to my right; wouldn't you know it: April and her friends from school were right there! A group of white chicks with attitude for miles.

"Kevin?! What are you doing over here? I thought you said you couldn't come over today?"

"I had to pick up my little cousin."

"Pick up your cousin from where?"

"From daycare."

"He goes to daycare around here?"

"Yes, my aunt works in lower Manhattan, sometimes I pick him up for her when she's running late."

"Do you want me to come with you?"

See there's two ways I could've handled that. One, take her by the daycare center that my cousin did actually go to. Or, two, fake a phone call from my aunt. I did the latter.

"Hello?—"

"Yes, I'll be there soon—

"I'm sorry—"

"I got caught up on the trains—"

"Tell them I'll be there in 10 minutes—"

"Alright, sorry Auntie—"

I "hung up" the phone.

"That was my aunt… She's steaming. I have to leave. I'm mad late. Plus, my little cousin would snitch if he saw me with you. I don't want my aunt to think you were the reason I was late. I want my family to like you."

"*Aw*, baby, it's okay. I'll call you later."

She kissed me goodbye.

I walked not even half a block before Allegra called me.

"I just got off the bus. Where are you?"

Shit…that was a close one.

"I'm coming your way right now. I had to stop at the store real quick."

"Okay." She replied.

The walk back to the bus stop was cool. In my mind I tried to figure out what Allegra was really up to. The pizza shop was just a meet-up point. Maybe the movies or something? I don't know. It was suspicious, but a good suspicious. It kept me wondering. All my wondering had taken me three blocks in about two minutes. I made it to the bus stop. There she was.

"Shall we get some stanky pizza, Kevin?" she said.

"Pizza? C'mon, what's the real plan?"

"Umm…I just wanted to get some pizza," she replied.

"You brought me all the way out here for some pizza

neither of us like?"

"Okay…Maybe not. Just follow me, gosh."

"Oh, boy. Whatever you say, mom."

She smiled.

Allegra had a beautiful smile. Not just any beautiful smile, but a shy, gorgeous smile. Her eyes were two blue diamonds. But they had some mileage on them. I could see some pain, and the insecurities.

"We're gonna go to my favorite spot in Brooklyn. Okay? And don't tell anyone about this place. Okay?" She said, earnestly.

"And where's that?" I asked.

"Do you know where Dumbo is?"

"Yeah."

"Ever been to Brooklyn Bridge Park?"

"I don't think so."

"Good. Your first time can be special."

"Are we still talking about the park, or—?"

"Kevin, *shutup!*" She blushed and laughed.

"You know how to get there from here?"

"Just follow me."

I could tell we were headed for the 9th street train station. It was a block away and Allegra already started to walk at a diagonal. Guess she was trying to cross me up.

"Oh, so we're taking the train?"

"Oh, my gosh, you do have a brain after all," she said, as she bit her lips and arched her eyebrows.

"Ha, very funny."

We entered through the north end of the station at around 6:50. I swiped my metro card through first, and

Allegra followed. We climbed the steps at an even pace as Allegra continued to make some more jokes. She was funny and cute like that. Borderline goofy. I liked how she could be herself around me. That was a major difference between Allegra and April. April always tried too hard to fit. She'd always be competing with everyone else for attention, over the simplest things.

"Kevin, what's your favorite color?" Allegra asked.

"Metallic silver," I replied. "You?"

"Oh, mine's Forest Green."

"Forest Green?" I laughed. "That's interesting."

"What?! I like trees. Who likes *metallic silver*?"

"I do."

"Oh, that's interesting." She said, mocking me.

I kissed her—

"What was that for?" she asked.

"I don't know. Just felt like it, I guess."

"Well, feel like it again. It was nice."

This time, we kissed longer. When we opened our eyes, we noticed a middle-aged couple watching us, smirking.

"You two look cute together," the woman said.

Allegra and I looked at one another, and smiled back at the lady.

"Thank you." We said, simultaneously.

"I remember when I was younger, I had a cute relationship like yours."

Just then, her husband, boyfriend or whoever, motioned for her to stop.

"Baby, let them kids be." He said.

"What? What did I do? Leave me alone." She said.

I could smell the liquor on her breath. He smiled.

That awkward pushover smile I'd seen in my mother's eyes before. He was embarrassed. Thankfully, the train pulled into Atlantic Avenue. I smiled at the couple, then I cradled Allegra's waist.

"Well, have a nice day," I said to the couple.

"You, too." They said.

Allegra and I began walking towards the staircase to transfer to the 3 train when I felt her hand clawing to reach mine. She had reached to hold my hand, so I obliged.

We made it to the top of the stairs, hand in hand, until we reached the train platform.

"Which stop are we getting off?" I asked.

"Clark Street, I think." She replied.

"Cool." I said.

The train came almost immediately, and we got on and found a seat near one of the subway maps.

"What time do you have to be home?" I asked.

"Oh, my mother doesn't care. Whenever I'm ready, I guess."

She sounded worried, sad even.

"What do you mean she doesn't care?"

"It's nothing."

"You alright?" I asked.

"Yeah, I'm fine." She said. "What time do you have to be home?"

"Well I'm trying to get home by 9."

"What's at 9?" She asked.

"The Yankees game."

"Ew. You're a Yankees fan?"

"Since I was 3...Is there a problem miss?" I said with a smile.

"No, sir. No problem."

"Who's your favorite team?' I asked.

I was hoping she didn't say the Mets. If she said the Mets, it was over right there.

"I don't really watch baseball," she said.

Whew. That was a close one.

"So why'd you say 'Ew?'" I asked.

"Just messing with ya," she said, laughing.

The train pulled into Clark Street. We got off the train and walked up stairs. We got to the top of the stairs and saw the two exits and didn't know which way to go.

"Do we go straight or to the right?" I asked.

"Um…I don't know."

"Come on…" I said, grabbing her hand and pulling her towards me as I walked straight.

When we came outside of the entrance, I looked right and left and proceeded to walk left. I remember coming to dumbo earlier in the year with my father, near where I think this park was supposed to be. So I just basically led the way to Dumbo in hopes that we'd find the park.

"So you came up with the plans and don't know where to go?" I said jokingly.

She laughed.

"My friend Sarah told me, but I forgot. She just told me what stop to get off. I didn't really know how to get there from here."

"You gotta be kidding me." We crossed the street.

"I'm sorry. I'm sorry."

"It's gonna take a lot more than a sorry."

"Here's a kiss!" she said. Then gave me a nice one. "Are we good, now?"

"That works," I replied, taking in how good her lips felt.

After more kissing in the middle of the sidewalk, we walked west. We had to be going in the right direction because I saw Grimaldi's, and knew that was close to the bridge.

"I think it's down there," she said pointing in front of us.

"Oh, really? So now you know where we're going?" I asked.

We both laughed.

"Shutup. Just keep walking down there," she said.

We walked about three blocks until we got down to this cobbled road. Now we were really lost. We just followed the crowd and made a left. As we started walking we could smell the water. O.K., we were close. We made another right and we were a block away from grass.

"See, I told you!" She said.

"Told me what?"

"To keep going straight, duh!"

"But we *didn't* keep going straight. We had to make a left and a right, remember? I got us here."

"Yeah, yeah."

She grabbed my hand again, and we walked down a passageway of dirt and rocks until we found a nice spot in the grass amid the sunset. It was well after 7 o'clock now, and the sun had already begun to set. We sat down in a shared silence. In the distance, the water and rocks picture must've formed the same picture in our heads.

"Kevin…"

"Allegra?" I said, matching her tone.

"I don't want this day to end."

I winked at her, and kissed the top of her head. "I don't want this day to end either."

"Are you going to break up with April?"

I paused for a second.

"I like you, Kevin. There's something about you. I don't know what it is. But I know I don't want to share you with another girl."

"Well, I—"

"And I don't want April to be hurt either."

"I hear you." Even though I liked Allegra and was ready to break up with April, I wasn't quite sure if I was ready to break up with April's neighborhood.

"So what are we going to do?"

"I'm supposed to go over to April's house tomorrow. I'll let her know what's up."

Get Rid of the Kid

I could still hear the sirens blaring behind me. But I kept walking. I had to pace myself. I had five minutes until the fire department showed up, and I knew Phil's moms would be home soon. I had three blocks to go until I reached Thompson's park. I had to get my bag and get the fuck out of town. My train was leaving at midnight, which meant I only had an hour and some change to get from Brooklyn to Penn Station.

Under normal circumstances, I wouldn't have taken so many chances. But I had to. And now, there were cops everywhere. And in order to get my stash and go-bag that I had hidden in the park, I was going to have to walk through them.

"Excuse me," this burly, light skinned cop said. "Do you live around here?"

"No, I'm just on my way to the park. I play ball for the Bed Stuy AAU basketball team. We had a tournament earlier, and I left my bag at the park. I'm just going to get it."

"All right, but you're going to have walk on the other side of the street. There's a police investigation going on.

"No problem. What happened?" I asked.

"There's been a shooting."

"Wow."

"Yeah, so I'm not sure you want to be walking around here right about now."

"Who you telling—"

"So get your bag from the park, do whatever you gotta do, and get home. Might be some gang stuff going on. You don't need to get caught up in that."

"I hear you, thank you officer."

I crossed the street walking at a steady pace. I wanted to run, or at least fast-walk. But I didn't want to draw any attention to myself. There were two dark blue, unmarked detective cars, and I don't know how many squad cars parked at crazy angles in front of Phil's house. I was almost at the corner, when I was stopped by a plain clothes DT.

"You know what happened here tonight?" he said. He was fat and white with cheap black loafers on.

"Heard somebody got shot," I replied, half-way between a walk and a stop.

"That's what I heard to. You know who did it?" he pressed.

I knew he didn't know anything. That's just how cops are, they press everybody. And if you're black, and near the scene of a crime, they automatically assume you either did it or know who did. "No, sir. I have no clue what went on here tonight. I was playing in a basketball tournament earlier. I'm just on my way to the park."

"You said, you sell drugs in the park?"

"No, sir. I said I played ball earlier. I left my bag in the park. Just on my way to get it. My house keys are in it."

"Where do you live at?" he asked, shifting and trying to throw me off.

"Marcy!"

"You sell drugs in Marcy? What are you doing over here? If I check you right now, am I going to find drugs?"

"No, sir."

"I believe you. You look like a good kid...You know the fella that got shot? His name is Phillip Tanner?"

"Yeah, I know Phil?"

"How do you know Phil? You guys friends?" the officer asked, following his lead.

"Everybody know Phil. But I went to school with him. From Kindergarten up until 8th grade."

"Oh, yeah? You know him well. Guys used to hang out and get into trouble together?"

"Nah, we was cool when we were younger. He used to play ball, too. But then he started hanging with the wrong crowd."

He took out a small notebook and started to write in it.

"I'm going to need your name."

"My name is David."

"What's your last name?"

"Miller." My name was neither David or Miller.

"So, tell me about this crowd Phil started hanging around with."

He was hooked now. If I fed him enough good bullshit, I knew he'd let me go. So I kept with it.

"I don't know anybody by name. Some cats you see around the basketball games and stuff. But that's not my world. I'm trying to get a basketball scholarship...Can I go, now? My moms be buggin' when I come home late. I had to beg her to let me go to this tournament today."

"Yeah, I'll let you go in a minute. You got a phone?"

"I did. Ran out of minutes. I can give you my house phone number, or my coach's number."

I gave him a fake number of course. And there was no coach. There was a basketball tournament earlier, though. But I didn't come around here for that. I came to kill Phil.

"Listen. When you get home, give your mother my card. I'm Dectective Riley. Let her know that I'm going to need to speak to you and her."

Just then, his cell phone rang. "Hold on, David. Stay right there. I gotta take this."

When he got off the phone, he told me he just got the news from the hospital: Phil didn't make it.

As I crossed the corner to the park, I overhead a "10-53, victim DOA," being called in on Lynch and Harrison. That was right near Jen's apartment. I don't believe in coincidences. And a hit and run right on Jen's corner wasn't a coincidence. Only proved that I was right not to answer the phone when she called. I knew the "victim" was Jen. And it wasn't too hard to figure out that Mayor was behind it.

I got to the park, went to the bushes, and grabbed my bag. I thought about leaving my gun right there in the bushes. But if Jen was already dead, I knew Mayor's whole crew would be in the streets looking for me.

Coming out of the park, I flagged down a gypsey and got in. I told him that I was going to Manhattan, but to take the Williamsburg Bridge. We were driving up Bedford, almost at Myrtle, when a car came up alongside of us. I looked over, and it was Jen. She was signaling the cab driver to pullover. He didn't, instead, he sped up. Jen followed suit and came up on his side and pointed a gun at him. When he still didn' slow down, I reached into my bag, pulled out my gun, at put it to the back of his head.

"Pull over, motherfucker!"

He pulled over to the right. Jen pulled over behind him, and walked up to us. The cab driver put his hands up and turned to face Jen.

"Cory, get out the car," she said to me. I jumped out. The cab driver yelled "Don't shoot, Don't shoot!" Too late: Jen shot him twice in the head.

I was now with Jen, driving over the Williamsburg Bridge to Manhattan.

"Mayor put it on the wire to all the cab dispatches to look out for you. That Dominican motherfucker called it in where he picked you up at. You know Mayor sent me to get rid of you, right?"

I didn't answer. I figured as much.

"I saw you when you came on Phil's block. You were sloppy. I could've took you right there. You didn't even see me."

She was taking her time, talking with a measured tongue.

"But I let you live. You know why?"

I didn't reply.

"Cuz, there was an accident in front of my place a couple of hours ago. A pregnant women was killed. I saw the whole thing. The car she was in flipped over twice. Her and her baby were killed. She had a son with her. Little boy couldn't have been no more than 10 years old...Despite that car flipping over two times. He lived...I was leaving my building, on my way to come kill you. But there was something about that little boy. He wasn't crying. The EMS workers thought it might of been because of shock. But I looked into his eyes. He was there. He knew what was going on...So, I'm driving, and I'm thinking about this little boy, and the shit he's going to have to deal with growing up. And I thought to myself, I trade your life for his. So, I'm going to take you to Penn Station. I'm even going to give you some money. And you're going to leave New York. Then, I'm going to go back to Brooklyn, and I'm going to find that little boy. And I'm gonna look after him. And when he's 13, I'm going to teach him how to kill, just like I taught you."

Once over the bridge, I asked Jen to stop at a corner deli so that I could get a water and snacks for my train ride. When I came out of the store, for some reason, I couldn't help but think about the little boy she'd told me about, and how she was going to take care of him. Just then, I had a burning feeling in my gut, like the first time I killed someone. I got back into the car, and Jen smiled at me. She looked at me as if I had done her a favor.

"Did you get what you want?" She asked.

"No," I replied. Then, I shot her in the head, got out of the car, and caught a yellow cab to Penn Station.

The Affair of Agnes Miller

It was late afternoon, and English lit tutor, Agnes Miller, a short, good-spirited and attractive white woman in her mid-20s, sat at her living room table, tutoring Mercer, a handsome, black, precocious—but not obnoxiously so—16-year-old high school senior.

After the two finished up their day's tutoring session, Agnes watched as Mercer gathered his composition notebook and notes and placed them into his backpack. Mercer stood up from the table and put his backpack on. He remained standing, watching Agnes closely, as Agnes stood up. Mercer stepped towards her. He was almost a half a foot taller than her.

"See, I *knew* something was different! You got a new haircut," Mercer said.

Agnes smiled. Several days earlier, she had gotten new bangs.

"It looks good on you," he continued.

"You think?" she replied. Joe, her boyfriend, didn't even notice her new haircut.

Mercer gently touched Agnes' hair. They shared an awkward but comforting look.

"Yeah, I think it looks *real* good," Mercer said in a playful tone.

Agnes gave a defensive laugh. She was flattered and taken aback at the same time.

"Umm, ok. Get your head out of the gutter, Mercer. What's your next assignment?" She asked, quickly changing the mood.

"Oh, right. I forgot. My bad...We have to do a book report on one of the books we read this semester."

"Oh, that sounds easy enough. Which book did you

pick?"

Mercer pulled out a copy of *Fahrenheit 451*.

"I chose this book by this Bradbury guy."

Agnes began to laugh.

"Ha! "*This Bradbury guy*." Well, that Bradbury Guy is a pretty important American author, Mercer. A *Fahrenheit 451* is a classic."

"Yeah, that's what I hear. But I only chose his book because Truffaut made it into a film. I liked the film better," replied Mercer.

Agnes couldn't believe it. "*Really*?" she said.

Agnes took her seat back at the table. Mercer, followed suit, sat down as well.

"I mean, the book was cool, too. But Truffaut brought it alive, you know. I think his film interpretation was similar to how I imagined things in the book."

"Oh, yeah, How so? Give me an example," she said.

"In the film, Clarisse looks like I thought she would. She has short brown hair, and she's pretty. In the book, I didn't get much of a read on how she looked. I guess she was pretty. I just couldn't quite picture her."

"I see." Agness replied. She'd often thought about Clarisse as well.

"Another thing I liked about the film is the way Truffaut showed the world that they lived in."

"What do you mean? Their time, society?"

"Yeah, you know, I get the whole utopian society thing and the way Bradbury was making a commentary on how he saw stuff turning out in the country, but Truffuat was more subtle with it."

Agnes liked the way Mercer expressed himself. She enjoyed talking with him.

"I agree. Bradbury was kind of heavy handed with his message. But he was making an important point.

"I guess so... And one more thing about the film, I thought Clarisse and Montag were gonna get together. In the book, I didn't get the same sense. Well, at least not as much."

Agnes' eyes widened. "Well, I haven't seen the film. But Yes! When I read the book the first time in high school, I thought the same thing. It never materialized, but I felt the tension was there."

The room got quiet for about two beats. Then, Mercer spoke up.

"I agree...Anyway, so what do you think I should write about for my essay? We either have to compare two characters from the book that we choose, or do some other kind of analysis."

"Oh, that sounds cool. Why don't you do a comparative analysis of the book and the film?"

"I see, like a comparison between the relationship Clarisse and Montag have in the book vs. the film?"

"Yeah, something like that."

"Right, *right*... I like that. I can dig it."

"When's your paper due?"

A small cloud of gloom fell over Mercer's face.

"In three weeks. And I have to get at least a B on it to raise my final grade for the class. 'Member, I'm trying to go on this trip to Paris. Did you forget?"

Agnes smiled. Of course she remembered.

"Yes, yes, I know Mercer, your big trip to the young filmmakers workshop in Paris. How could I possibly forget? It shouldn't be too hard to get a B if you apply what we've gone over these past couple of months."

"I hope so. I'm not missing that trip."

"You'll do fine."

Mercer put his copy of *Fahrenheit 451* back into his bookbag and once again began his departure.

"All right, Miss Miller. That about wraps it for today."

Agnes smiled at Mercer. She thought it was cute how he called her 'Miss Miller.' At 26, was she really that old? she thought to herself.

"Yes, we're finished. Get out of here," she said.

"Hey, you eat yet? I'm about to go grab a meal. You wanna roll?"

Agnes patted Mercer on his back.

"Nice try, Mercer. But I don't think my boyfriend would like that. Plus, I think I'm too old for you."

"Aw, man, it's cool. But you know, in Europe, that type of thing isn't frowned upon.... Yo, you know you gonna miss me when I go to Paris."

"Well, one thing at a time, Mercer. If you don't do well on your essay, you won't be going anywhere, Mr," she retorted.

"Ah, funny lady… All right, then. I'm outta here."

They walked to the door.

"See you next week!"

"See ya, Mercer," she replied, closing the door behind him.

After Mercer left, Agnes straightened up the living room a little bit. Her roommate, Gabby, would be home soon. She pushed the living room table back to it's original spot, gathered some papers, then headed to her bedroom. Having finished straightening up the place, she went into the kitchen for a snack and some water. Just then, Gabby walked in.

"Honey, I'm home," Gabby yelled sarcastically.

"I'm in the kitchen, Gabbs," Agnes replied in a soft yell.

Gabby, a tallish, pretty and fit blond, put her things down in the living room and joined Agnes in the kitchen.

"Hey, I ran into that kid you tutor in the lobby."

Agnes grabbed her pretzels and water bottle then

walked back into the living room. She blushed at Gabby's mentioning of Mercer.

"Who, Mercer?" Agnes asked rhetorically.

"Yes, I like totally have a crush on him," Gabby replied.

"I know, right. Me too."

They both laughed.

"That kid's gonna be a freakin' lady killer when he grows up," Gabby added.

"Gabby! He's only 16!" Agnes exclaimed.

"Oh, so what. He looks older for his age. Anyway, it's different guys and older girls."

Just then, Gabby's phone began to ring. Gabby answered her phone, it was her date for the night.

"Yeah, yeah I'm coming, I'm coming. Just give me a half-an-hour," she said, rushing him off the phone.

"That guy is such a nag!" Gabby said, visibly irritated by the pestering call.

"Oh, please, shutup, you know you like the attention," Agnes replied.

"O.K., maybe I do, just a little—"

They laughed.

"And at least he is nagging you. I could do for some nagging from my freakin' boyfriend."

"What about you? You and Joe still going out tonight? Hey, maybe we can double date?"

"Maybe, I don't know. He said we have reservations at 8."

"Where are you guys going?"

"I don't know yet. He told me earlier that it's a surprise."

Just then, Agnes' phone rang. It was Joe.

"Wait, speak of the devil...Gabbs, hold on."

Misery fell across Agnes' face, as she listened to Joe

cancel their date once again.

"But I thought we were going to go out tonight...What do you mean?... I understand...No, I understand, Joe... Raincheck then....Ok...Love you, too, Bye."

Agnes hung up the phone, crushed.

"Don't tell me he's not coming? He's standing you up again? Wow, that guy's a real tool. Don't let him get you down," Gabby said.

"Looks like I have a date with the couch and Netflix," Agnes said, trying to appear as if she wasn't hurt. Her eyes became glossy, but she didn't quite cry.

"Do you want to go out with me and my guy? He won't mind." Gabby offered.

"No, I don't want to tag along and be a third wheel. No, you go out, have a good time."

"You sure? Trust me, it's not a problem."

"I'm sure."

"Say, I know!"

"What?" Agnes asked.

"Why don't you call Mercer?" Gabby said jokingly.

"Shut up!" Agnes said with a laugh.

Gabby left the room and started to get ready for her date. Agnes stayed in the living room on the couch, moping with her pretzels and water bottle. She was thinking about her relationship with Joe, and finally coming to terms with the reality that they no longer had a real relationship . How could you love someone who you don't see much? Plus, more and more now, it just seemed like Joe was avoiding her, she thought.

***

It had been three weeks since his last tutoring session with Agnes, and Mercer arrived early. He had good news to tell her, so he rushed over right after school.

Upstairs in their apartment, Agnes was getting dressed, and Gabby was preparing to leave for work.

"K, Agnes, I'm gone." Gabby yelled from the front door."

"All right. Hey, listen, could you put those crates outside in the hallway for me. The Super's supposed to come by and get them," Agnes yelled back from her bedroom.

"Oh, O.K." Gabby began moving the four empty milk crates into the hallway. Upon carying out the last one, Mercer appeared.

"Oh, hey, Mercer. I heard your footsteps coming up the stairs. I thought you were the Super. The door's open, you can go right in."

"Oh, okay cool, cool… thank you."

Mercer entered the apartment. Agnes was nowhere to be seen. And the living room table was empty, no books or writing materials were on it like usual. He started to take his bookbag off, when Agnes entered the living room wearing nothing but a white robe. They both stood there shocked. wet hair and slippers. Agnes had no idea that Gabby had let Mercer in; and Mercer had know idea that Agnes had recently finished taking a shower.

"Mercer!" Agnes exclaimed, red face and all. "Um, you're early."

"Oh, wow. My bad. I didn't get a slice after school and stuff. I just came straight over. When I came upstairs, your roommate let me in." Mercer couldn't help but look at Agnes' legs and bare feet.

Agnes felt embarrassed, but not uncomfortable.

"Um, O.K., ok, give me a moment…You can grab a water from the fridge if you like. Excuse me—"

Agnes left the room. Mercer sat down at the table and pulled his materials out, getting ready for the session. All he could think about was Agnes in her robe.

Agnes returned to the living room fully dressed in nicely fitting black yoga pants, a t-shirt, and running sneakers. This was no better. The yoga pants turned Mercer on even more than the robe had.

"So, how did you do on your essay?" Agnes asked, acting as if Mercer did not just see her standing there in a robe.

"I got an A!" Mercer was excited to tell Agnes all about his success.

"No, kidding? That's fantastic, Mercer. See, I told you, you'd be fine."

"Un, hungh. And now I'm going to Paris, baby!!!"

Mercer was ecstatic.

"I'm happy for you," Agnes said.

All of a sudden, a look of gloom and sadness fell over Agnes' face, and she began to cry out of nowhere.

"What's wrong?" Mercer asked.

"Nothing, nothing...Oh, my gosh. I'm sorry. Excuse me."

Agnes left the room and went to the bathroom. Inside, she gathered up some cold water and splashed her face several times. Then she wiped her face with a towel, gathered herself, and rejoined Mercer in the living room.

"Yo, Miss Miller, what was that about? Everything all right?"

"I'm sorry, Mercer. It's nothing."

"Come on, you can tell me." Mercer said.

"I think it's just ... I don't know. You're happy; you're going to Paris. And I'm happy for you, too. But I'm not happy with some things in my life at the moment. That's all. And I don't know why, but it just hit me at that moment."

Agnes started to choke up again.

"Why aren't you happy? What's wrong?" Mercer asked.

"Career stuff. And my idiot, so-called boyfriend. Things aren't the same anymore. I don't know why. But I can feel he's drifted away from me."

"I've been there before, yo. Don't I know it. I remember sophomore year, I was going out with this girl, and the same thing happened to me. She just drifted away. But I think it had something to do with me hooking up with her cousin. Maybe that was it, I don't know," Mercer said, laughing.

"Ha! You moron," Agnes replied with a small chuckle. "Listen, you know what, Mercer, would you mind coming back next week? I'm just not up for tutoring right now."

"Yeah, it's cool. I understand."

"Thanks."

Mercer scooped his stuff into his bookbag, got up from the table, and headed for the door.

"Cheer up, Miss Miller. Things work out for the right people."

"That's sweet, Mercer. Thank you."

Mercer left. A distraught, confused, Agnes walked into her kitchen and grabbed some water before she headed into her room. Once in her room, Agnes layed down on her bed, turned on her T.V., and started to watch an episode of "The Mentalist". It wasn't long before she dozed off.

Agnes got up around 9 o'clock and took a shower. Just after she got dressed, Gabby came home.

"Agnes!" she yelled out.

"I'm in the back…" Agnes yelled back.

Gabby could hear it in Agnes' voice. She didn't know what was wrong, but she knew something was up. When she entered the room her worries were reassured.

"Sweetie, what's wrong?" Gabby asked.

Agnes was fighting the tears again.

"Everyone's happy except me. You're happy, you met some amazing new guy, who can't wait to see you. Mercer's about to go off to fuckin' Paris. And my excuse for a boyfriend won't pick up his damn phone."

"You know, you don't need a guy to make you happy," Gabby replied.

"Yeah, I know, but why won't he call me back? Just fucking call back! He's probably bangin' some bimbo."

The look on Gabby's face changed from concern to fear.

"You know, Agnes...I've been meaning to talk to you about something…Actually, I feel that I have to tell you something."

"Yeah, what is it?" Agnes asked.

"You know this new guy that I've been seeing?"

Agnes sat up now, her back against the wall. She was confused as to why Gabby was hesitating.

"Yeah…" Agnes said.

"It's Joe." Gabby said softly.

The room fell silent for a moment, as Agnes tried to process what she'd just heard.

"Joe…Joe who?…Wait, my joe?!"

"Agnes, I didn't mean for it to happen, I swear. It started off as a friendship, I didn't mean for any of this to happen. It just did-"

Agnes gave a small laugh to herself, the way one does when they can't believe what they've just heard. "Wait, I'm here sitting in my bed sulking because my boyfriend keeps avoiding me, and you're the fucking reason why? You're my best friend!" Agnes said.

"I know, Agnes. Believe me, I'm so, so sorry. I didn't want it to be this way. I just wanted you—"

"Wow," Agnes cut her off. "I just… I-I have no words. You fucking cunt! I can't believe you'd do this to me! I don't believe this shit—"

"I'm sorry… It's been killing me. You have no idea

how terrible I feel. I feel like shit inside." Gabby said, now in tears.

Agnes wasn't trying to hear it.

"Un hungh, well, you should, Gabby! You should feel like shit, because that's what you are."

"Agnes, I'm so sorry."

"Well, you know what? You can be sorry somewhere else. I want you out of my apartment."

"Agnes, I'm sor—."

"GABBY. GET THE FUCK OUT OF HERE!!!"

Gabby dropped her head in shame, and walked out of Agnes' bedroom. Later that night, Gabby moved out.

It was two months later.

Agnes was sitting on the couch doing some Saturday morning reading when there was a knock on her door. Agnes walked to the door barefoot in grey sweatpants and a white tanktop. She thought it was Gabby coming by to pick up the last of her stuff. But when she opened the door, there stood Mercer.

"Hey, Miss Miller."

"Mercer!" Agnes exclaimed. She was happy to see him. He hadn't bothered to come back for their last tutoring sessions. "Come in, come in."

"Figured I aught to stop by before I left...Sorry for not coming to my last sessions."

"Oh, don't worry about it... So, the big trip to Paris, hungh? When are you leaving?"

"Later tonight."

"Oh, okay."

"You know I'm gonna miss you, right!" Mercer said with a smile.

"I'll miss our sessions, too. It was fun. I hope you learned a lot."

"No doubt."

Just then, Agnes' phone began to ring on the coffee table. She picked it up and sent it to voice mail, then she put her phone on silent.

"Not picking that up?" Mercer asked.

"It's my ex…" she said, clearly annoyed by him calling.

"Oh, your 'ex?' He's your ex now?" Mercer asked.

"Yeah, long story."

"I bet it is... Well, I just came by to shout you out before I left, Miss Miller." Mercer didn't really want to leave.

"Thank you. That was sweet of you...." There was an empty beat, then, "Say, Mercer, you can call me Agnes, you know."

"Oh yeah?" Mercer said, taking that as his cue .

"Yeah…"

Mercer leaned in and kissed her. When she didn't pull away, he wrapped his arms around her waist. Agnes threw her arms up and around his neck. Mercer put one hand on her ass. Agnes stepped back, and looked into Mercer's eyes. She kissed him softly on the cheek. Then she pulled her tanktop over her head and off. She grabbed Mercer's hand and led him back to her bedroom.

The Perfect Shot

A couple years ago, I attended a TedX talk for teens. I was a homeschooler amongst a sea of high schoolers, who had come together in large and small groups. I didn't really know anyone, and it was hard to make friends. Fortunately for me, there were a couple other homeschoolers in the house. The talk was held at a big theater space in the middle of Times Square. Every time I saw a new speaker come onto the stage, I thought I was watching a play.

During the intermission I went up to the stage and spoke with a few of the talkers. Then I headed out into the main hall and talked with a couple people and exchanged contact information.

Most of the girls I saw stayed in packs but I was able to pick off a couple stragglers. There was this one girl I met. I don't remember her name, but she was real pretty. In total, I got about six numbers and a couple e-mails. It was a successful day and the snacks were pretty tasty.

The talks were cool too. It was better than I expected. I wouldn't say any of the speakers were particularly inspirational but they dropped a couple useful jewels. But the real payoff came when I met Mr. Jenkins, the Editor-in-Chief for *Bullseye* magazine.

He gave me his business card and his personal e-mail in exchange for a promise. I had to make sure I contacted him within 72 hours. He said I had potential and real drive for a kid my age. I was 14 at the time. I really appreciated his offer because, after all, it was the only one I had.

Two years later, I was waiting outside his office for my first real assignment. I was the associate assistant camera holder. Which basically meant that I was the associate's, associate's, assistant camera holder's coffee-go-getter. Yeah, I know. At least I got paid for it. I worked on Tuesday's and Thursday's because those were the only available days in my curriculum. It worked out though, since I spent the rest of my week scouring the city for neat places to take pictures. I worked closely with the two main photojournalists on staff, Tucker and Hurley. They pretty much me taught me the ropes and told me to make sure I stayed out of their way.

The waiting room smelled like a tropical island. It was a mixture of women's perfume and Febreze air freshener. I was amazed at how well kept the office was on a consistent basis. The magazines on the big coffee table were aligned to perfection, the fax machines looked brand new, and there was always new art on the walls. Jenkins was a stickler for organization.

Today was my big day, or so I thought. I saw the look on Agatha's face, the receptionist, when I walked through the door. Agatha looked worried. Agatha was never worried. At least, I never saw it. She always had a smile on her face and tons of witty comments at her disposal.

But not today. Today Agatha was locked in her seat as if someone chained her there. Today, Agatha was scared of something and I don't know what it was. In my two years with the magazine, I'd never seen her like this. There must've been a problem with the last issue.

Last month, Tezlo CEO Seb Millner had been in town for a meeting with a group of shareholders. They were concerned about the recent large decline in Tezlo's stock price. Millner hadn't been seen in public for over four months. But this was different. He had to meet with shareholders, or face an uptick in sellers. Our magazine caught wind of Millner's meeting with his shareholders and invested in a stakeout.

Mr. Jenkins sent out Tucker and Hurley. The best. They brought me along because I promised to do food runs.

When Mr. Millner entered his hotel, they jumped into action. Hurley took the pictures of Millner, while Tucker did the brief interview. At first, I thought everything turned out fine. Hurley took some nice pictures of Millner, and far as I could tell, Tucker asked the right questions. Problem was, when the issue ran, the piece on Millner didn't go over as well as everyone hoped it would. In fact, the issue did poorly.

When the June issue of the magazine, the one with the piece on Millner in it, reached Mr. Jenkins' desk, it was all over. The June issue was bit of a flop, and there was a small dip in new subscriptions. For an entire week, Mr. Jenkins lashed out at everybody in the office for their lack of professionalism or any other fault that he could find. Nobody was spared.

During the same week, I overheard Rob, the Managing Editor, and Elliot, the Photo Editor, having an argument over the direction of the upcoming August issue that everyone was already working on. Elliot believed that *Bullseye* should just take a second stab at a photo-op with Millner and publish it in the next issue. He had gotten a tip that Millner would be at his Upper East Side home for the rest of the week, and so, why not get some new shots of him in his element? And that they could offer to run a correction to the original piece. Rob didn't think there was any point in trying. He also didn't think a correction was necessary, since the magazine hadn't technically gotten anything wrong. Being quoted out of context is certainly no cause for a correction, he thought. He further made it clear that what was done, was done, and that Jenkins had already made plans to hand out some pink slips.

I thought it was weird for Rob to take such a strong stance against making things better. But I let it go. After all, he was the Managing Editor, so he must've known best.

But there was something Elliot said that caught my attention. He said his source told him that Millner was going to be visiting the MET this afternoon to see his granddaughter. And that he'd be driving in a baby Blue Mercedes Benz, and that he'd most likely enter the museum discreetly through the employee entrance.

Elliot said this was the last time *Bullseye* would get a chance to interview Millner, let alone take his picture, and that it would be a great idea for *Bullseye* to send somebody over to the MET immediately. Rob didn't bite. He told Elliot it was a stupid idea. And Elliot left the office in a huff.

That's where I came in. I was going to do what Elliot was suggesting. I was going to take it upon myself to get that shot and that interview. But first I had to meet with Mr. Jenkins in 20 minutes to see if he needed me to run any errands.

"Jenkins would like to see you now," Agatha said.

I went into his office.

"Good afternoon, Chris, please take a seat," Mr. Jenkins said.

"How are you doing sir?" I asked.

"I'm fine."

"Now, Chris I'm sure you heard the June issue didn't turn out to well..."

I just nodded.

"Well, it appears we may have an opportunity to correct that situation. Rob tells me that his source gave him a tip that Millner will be at the MET this afternoon, visiting his granddaughter."

Rob told you this? I thought to myself.

"Now, Tucker and Hurley are on assignment in D.C. And I can't get a hold of Elliot, and his assistant is away. So, that leaves you. Here's what I need you to do for me."

I sat up in my chair in order to take notes.

"You won't need to write this down."

I put my pad away.

"I need you to get me the perfect shot by the end of the afternoon. Get me something of Millner, of course. But I also need one other solid shot that I can run for the piece called 'Fall in New York City.' Now, I know this is your first real assignment, but you should've learned enough working with Tucker and Hurley by now. And I trust you know what I expect from you."

"Yes, sir. I do. Thank you for the opportunity."

"I hope you do. Alright, get to work."

I exited his office, headed back through the waiting room and said goodbye to Agatha.

"Break a leg!" she yelled out.

I smiled.

Now I had two things to do. I had to get Jenkins his perfect shot, and I had to catch Millner on his way in or out of the museum.

When I got off the train a couple blocks away from the MET, I went inside the museum and stayed near the front desk so I could see everyone coming and going. I figured my best shot was catching Millner while he was leaving the museum.

Maxine was at the info desk as usual. She was gorgeous. I always wondered why she worked at a museum. With her looks, she could've earned a decent living, certainly more money than she was probably making working at the front desk of a museum. She was in her mid- to late 20s, and she had the prettiest of smiles. Whenever she saw me she'd always say hi, and talk me up a little. And I would always try to extend the conversation further. But something always came up. Unfortunately, our conversations never lasted as I would've like them to. Today was no different. Only I'd be the one cutting things short, on account I had to keep up with Millner.

"Hey, Chris. How are you?" she said.

"Hey, Maxine. I'm good. You?"

"No complaints... Say, I see you around here a lot," she said sarcastically.

"I like the art."

"No, really? You're like in here all the time. Why do you come here so much?" she said with her polite smile.

"The art helps me think. And today I need some inspiration."

"What for?"

"I work for this magazine, right. And my boss says I need to get *the perfect shot* by this afternoon."

The phone next to her started to ring.

I looked outside and saw a blue Mercedes Benz make a

turn onto one of the side blocks. Millner got out.

"I should probably get going actually," I said.

"Hope you get your shot," she replied.

I decided to go upstairs to the balcony to keep an eye on Millner. It wouldn't have been smart to attack Millner on his way into the museum. So I waited.

After ten minutes upstairs, I headed back down to see if Millner's car was still outside. It was. So I knew he was still here. When I left the museum, I noticed that another girl was covering the info desk. Maxine was gone.

I walked outside and sat on the museum steps. I wrote down a couple questions on my notepad for Millner, and waited for him to get out of the museum.

I felt a tap on my shoulder from behind. It was Maxine.

"Waiting for someone?" she asked.

"Oh, no. I'm just thinking." I said. As much as I would have like to talk with Maxine, I was concentrating on not losing Millner.

"What are you thinking about?" she asked.

Just then, I saw Millner walking across the street. Where he came from I have no clue. Must've been an employee entrance or something that I didn't know about. But he was only about 15 yards or so away. He turned around and looked back to the museum. Maxine waved to him. He blew her a kiss. The guy was twice Maxine's age. I heard about businessmen having young girlfriend's all the time, but Maxine didn't seem like the type to fall for Millner. Still, Maxine's face was lit up with joy. I guess she was the type after all.

"You know Seb Millner?" I asked.

"Yes. He's my grandfather," she said.

"Oh, he's your *grandfather*," I said relieved.

"Yeah, what did you think?"

"Ha! Hold on, I'll be right back, give me a second."

I darted down the museum steps in pursuit of Mr. Millner and his car. Just before he pulled off I knocked on the window.

Millner let his window down. I caught my breath.

"Excuse me Mr. Millner, I'm sorry to bother you. I'm a good friend of Maxine's. She told me it would be all right to say hello to you."

"Hello, young man," he said. He sounded pleasant, not at all harsh like he was often described.

"I'm also an assistant photojournalist with *Bullseye* magazine. I was hoping I could take your picture, and ask you just a few quick questions. It would mean a lot to me."

"Questions? I already gave an interview to your magazine. And if I recall, I was terribly misquoted."

"Yes, I know sir… I learned today that we're going to run a correction and a new favorable piece on you for the August issue."

"Favorable?"

"Yeah, it's an issue on 'Fall in New York.' Everybody knows your favorite time in New York is the fall." I really didn't know if this was his favorite time in New York or not.

"Well, that's true. The fall is my favorite time in New York."

"I won't take no more than five minutes of your time."

"You're a friend of my granddaughter's?"

"Yes, sir. She's the nicest person I know." She really was.

He exhaled. Then, "Get in! You've got five minutes. I'm on my way to the Polo Mansion to buy some shirts. This is the only time I get to myself."

After I wrapped up my brief interview with Millner, I took a few pictures of him inside and outside of his car and headed back to the museum. I'd gotten all I needed.

I jogged back to the museum steps, Maxine remained in the same spot I left her, confused.

"What did you need to talk with my grandfather about?" She asked.

"I'm a photojournalist with *Bullseye* magazine. I was doing a follow-up interview on your grandfather for our next issue."

"Oh. Is everything okay?"

"Yeah, everything's cool. I've got to get back to the office, though, and file my report." I liked when I said, *file my report.* It made me feel like a professional. "But I'll be back later in the week."

"Somehow, I'm sure you will."

She smiled.

With Millner's interview in hand and a museum date with Maxine later in the week, my afternoon was already a success. Still, I hadn't eaten yet, and I needed some fuel.

After I ate and had some time to think, my mind was full of all these ideas for pictures. I thought of maybe going to soho to take a couple shots of the graffiti that lay near the tattoo shops. I even considered setting up a shot near the empire state building. But that would've been too typical and

Jenkins would've exploded. So I went back to the drawing board. Maybe I could take a quick trip to Central Park and snap a couple pictures of some trees and make my pictures look real artsy. I was troubleshooting some ideas but nothing was really sticking. I was racing against the clock, so I had to think fast.

Just then, I saw a vagrant with her child. All they had with them was a few bubble coats for sleeping, a cardboard sign that read, *Help please, trying to get back on my feet*, and a jar with a couple dollars and coins in it. The woman just looked at me, curious as to why I stopped in my tracks.

I didn't know how she would take it or if she would even allow me, but I thought this would make a great shot.

"Here, Miss I have $10 but that's all I have," I said, placing money in her cup.

"Do you mind if I take a picture of you and your daughter as well?"

Her daughter was asleep. She was about 3 or 4 years old, so she didn't really understand what I was saying anyway. But she woke up for a second and looked up at her mother to see what her response would be. Her mother opened her mouth to speak.

"What do you want to take our picture for?" She asked.

There was a stench coming from her mouth and her daughter that would put a lot of people off. But it didn't bother me. I just felt sorry for the woman and her daughter. It had to be hard living a life like that for who knows how long. Their eyes told a story that I thought deserved to be captured on my camera.

"It's for a magazine," I said.

"Oh, a magazine? Why didn't you say so! I use to be a model you know. Give me a second, while I find my headband."

I held my camera in amazement as this homeless woman searched for a hairband to put her hair up. She looked into her grey Nike gear bag that was white once. The logo was faded and every inch of material was smothered in dirt. Then she looked in an old bean jar where she kept coins. After that failed she looked behind the gate she had her back on to see if it had fell behind her. Finally, she found a dirty pink headband that was lying underneath her daughter and put it in her hair. Somehow her hair remained still in a bun with a couple strands slipping out here or there. But she was ready for her photo shoot.

"How do I look?"

"You look fan-tastic!"

Her daughter kept looking at me with one eye opened as she tried to sleep. She didn't really know what was going on. She was just really engaged in that nap of hers.

"Cmon sweetie, wake up. This young man is going to take our picture for a magazine."

Her daughter's eyes widened and she sprung into action. She wiped her face with a dirty paper towel that looked like it'd been used a thousand times for other engagements.

"How do I look, mommy?" she asked.

"You look beautiful, honey."

"Doesn't she look beautiful?" she asked me.

"Yes, very. You're a very pretty little girl—"

"What's your name?" the mother asked me.

"Chris."

"Oh, that's such a sweet name. My name's Susan. And

this princess here is Abby. Say hi, Abby."

"Hi."

"Nice to meet you two."

After I took about seven shots I was on my way. I picked up my notepad, put the cap back on my camera and got ready to head back to the office. I figured I'd gotten enough to hand in a perfect shot.

"When do I get to see the pictures?" Susan asked.

"I'm at the MET all the time. So I'm around here. If you're usually around here, I'll bring you a copy of the magazine when it comes out."

"Oh, that's nice. Don't forget to tell me if Vogue needs me again."

I laughed. I wondered if she actually was in Vogue at one point in her life.

"I'll be sure to let you know."

I walked off, on my way back to the office. I had a couple hours to spare, so I took the long way.

On my way back to the office I took in the city and everything it had to offer. I thought of what it would be like to finally have a real title at *Bullseye* magazine. I could finally move up and have my own office space instead of sharing with all the other interns. Maybe Jenkins would give me a shot to take pictures on the big jobs. By 20, maybe I'd make it to Assistant Photo Editor.

It all depended on my pictures and the interview I did with Millner. Hopefully it was enough to remind Jenkins why he gave me a job in the first place. For my drive and all.

I headed to Central Park.

When I strolled into Central Park I had two more hours to go until the clock hit four. I wanted to get a couple shots of some New Yorkers in action. I'd title this part of my catalog, "The City in Motion." I knew Jenkins would really dig that idea. He liked that kind of shit.

After I walked through Central Park for about ten minutes, I realized I hadn't really gotten much. There were people in the park like always but there was still something missing. I didn't feel like I was getting what I wanted so I continued to walk.

I walked past the Shakespeare in the Park ticket booth. I remembered the last time I spent a summer day in the blazing heat with my summer camp. The show was good, but the heat that day was unbearable. A girl waiting in line for Shakespeare in the Park tickets stopped me.

"Hey!" she said.

"Hey, what's going on," I replied. There was something about this girl that was really familiar. I don't know if it was the clothes, the voice, or the hair, but there was something about her that I couldn't quite put my finger on.

"Don't I know you from somewhere?" she asked.

"What's your name?"

"Chris. You look familiar, too."

We laughed.

"I'm Carla." She put out her hand.

I shook her hand. "Good to meet you, again, Carla."

She laughed.

"Yeah, right? I don't know what it is either."

I scanned Carla's eyes again and ran her face through my head. I went through different cycles of thought. I tried to see if I knew Carla from school, maybe photography classes or some workshop we might've been in together. Then it hit me!

"You didn't go to high school; you homeschooled, right?" I asked.

"Yeah, how'd you know?"

"You were at this TedX talk like two years ago—"

"Oh, yeah, THAT'S it!"

"Yeah! I remember you. I think I still have your e-mail in my phone. How've you been?"

Carla was pretty before from what I remembered. But now she was really something. Her hair was longer and straight. And she was a couple inches taller. She had on a nice flower dress and a pearl necklace, both look good on her golden complexion.

"I've been good. Working my way up at this magazine."

She laughed.

"What do you do there?"

"I'm a photojournalist actually."

"A photojournalist? Wow, but you look so young," she said with a laugh.

"I started early."

"How'd you get the job?"

"Do you remember the guy from *Bullseye* magazine? The guy everyone wanted his autograph afterwards?"

"You work for *Bullseye* magazine!?"

I smiled. "No doubt…After Mr. Jenkins finished giving out autographs to the students around him, I went up to him and told him about how much I loved photography. He gave me his business card, and 72 hours later I had an internship."

Carla's parents returned from the Shakespeare in the Park ticket booth and joined us. She introduced them to me. Her mother was white and her father was black. I had a feeling that Carla was mixed. Her mother remembered me from TedX, and she smiled a lot. Her father, however, studied my every move. Clara kept blushing and asking me questions.

"I just got an idea. Carla, can I take a picture of you for my magazine?"

"Of course," she said.

Surprisingly, Carla's father didn't object. So Carla and I went about 10 yards away.

"Honey, don't go to far," Carla's mother said.

When I looked through the viewfinder of my camera I felt like I was photographing a J Crew model. Carla was a natural. She moved freely from side to side with each pose.

"Let me see that pretty smile," I called out.

"This one?" she giggled.

"Yeah, that's it."

After ten more shots, I had enough pictures. I told her I'd try my best to get one of the shots into the magazine, but either way, I promised her copies of all the shots that I'd taken. Carla gave me her number and told me to make sure that I called her later. She didn't have to tell me twice.

I said goodbye to Carla and her parents, then I headed out of Central Park. I wasn't too far away, so I could hear Carla's mother mention my name. I don't know what she said, but I know that they were talking about me. Her mother liked me, I could tell. But her father seemed to have something against me. I think it had something to do with me being black.

I started walking to the train station. I was cruising through walk signal after walk signal until I hit a green light. There was a hot dog man strolling down the block where I stood. A woman crossed the street in between cars and headed for the dental office behind me. I saw a kid running down the block flying like superman. Then, I saw a police officer atop a horse near another entrance of Central Park.

The officer was in the middle of a conversation with a tourist who asked for directions. He was so into his conversation with the tourist he didn't see what I saw. His horse looked like it was crying. This big, brown horse, was standing there with the saddest eyes I'd ever seen.

I fumbled with my camera cap as I rushed to capture this moment. The water built up in the eyes of this beautiful horse gave me chills. I felt bad for the horse, I wish I could help, but all I could do was take a picture. The policeman's feet were in the shot but the horse looked up at me and stared right at the lens until I was finished. It was as if it was asking for help with its eyes. It was a beautiful shot.

On my way back to the office I had all these conflicting thoughts. I wanted to use the picture of the horse to further my career but at the same time I didn't. That horse spoke to me in a way. I couldn't just give that picture away for a job. I wanted to keep it for myself. When I looked up, I saw the cop looking at me. I smiled and made a b-line for the train station. I didn't like the suspicious look he was giving me.

Either way it went, Jenkins was going to like what I brought back to him. He didn't expect me to go out and get a follow up interview with Millner, and he certainly didn't expect me to find *Bullseye* magazine a new teen model. I'd done all of this in one afternoon, and surely this would be enough. At least I hoped it would be enough.

When I got back to the office, it was a little after 4pm. The office was empty and silent. Of course, Agatha was still there.

"You got your pictures?" she whispered, as I approached her desk.

"Yeah, I've got them right here. Why is it so quiet?"

"Jenkins had a meltdown. Elliot was fired. And other people were sent home on a forced vacation."

Rob took Elliot's idea, I figured he must've thrown him under the bus as well.

"Fired? What for?"

"I don't know. Something happened with him and Rob. Jenkins told him he was no longer needed."

I shook my head.

"Can I go in to see Mr. Jenkins? He told me to see him as soon as I got back."

"Yeah, sure. Go ahead."

His door was open, but I knocked anyway.

"Who is it?" He yelled out, turning around his chair.

"Oh, Chris. Come in."

Mr. Jenkins had his tie off half way in the garbage can near his desk. His shirt was unbuttoned at the top and his forehead was sweating. There were a number of papers scattered across his desk and dozens more crumpled up in the garbage cans nearest the door.

"Are you alright, Mr. Jenkins?" I asked.

He hesitated. Mr. Jenkins never hesitated.

"I'm fine. You got those pictures?"

"Yes, I have them right here on my Nikon."

"Let me see 'em."

Now I had a decision to make. I could let Mr. Jenkins see the shot I'd taken of the police horse or, I could just show him the shots of Millner, the homeless woman, and Carla, along with the brief interview I did with Millner.

"I saw Mr. Millner outside of the MET today."

Mr. Jenkins sat back in his chair and waited for me to continue.

"I was able to get a follow up interview and a couple pictures."

"You were huh? What did he say?"

"I just got him to speak on where he thinks mobile is going, and why he values his shareholders."

Mr. Jenkins wasn't giving me any indication that what I did was right. In fact, he didn't have much of a reaction at all. I hoped it meant that he was just processing everything I had to say in order to give me a proper response.

"I have my notes right here." I said.

"Let me see."

I handed Mr. Jenkins my notes, then I sat down and continued to watch his every move. He picked up his tie and put it back on. He buttoned one of his top buttons and adjusted his seat.

"You've done good, Chris. Very good, young man. You're going places around here."

"Thank you, Mr. Jenkins."

Mr. Jenkins was genuinely happy with my work but he was composed as well.

"And the pictures?" he said.

I was comfortable with not showing him the pictures of

the crying horse for two reasons. One, it seemed like the news I delivered hit home. Mr. Jenkins was in a good mood again and he was happy with my Millner interview. That alone could've gotten me a promotion. Two, I wanted to hold on to those pictures of the horse for something else. In the meantime, I'd keep those pictures for myself. Just didn't seem right to give them away. They were my best work yet.

"Here," I said, holding my camera up for Mr. Jenkins' to look into the viewfinder. I was careful to show him only the shots of Millner, Carla, and the homeless woman and her daughter.

All told, I took about 30 shots throughout that afternoon. Most of the pictures I took were of Carla. I knew Jenkins would really like those because they would work well with the youth section of the magazine.

He finished cycling through my pictures.

"Very good, Chris. I like what I see."

"Thank you, Mr. Jenkins."

"You're growing into a very mature photographer. I believe you're going to go a long way as a photojournalist."

"Thank you."

"That being said, I think you should come in tomorrow so we can discuss giving you a new position. Unfortunately, Elliot has left us. And I'm promoting his assistant, Sloan. She will be the new Photo Editor. I'd like to talk to the two of you together about you being her assistant."

I did it!

"Thanks a lot, Mr. Jenkins. That's great news."

He smiled and nodded his head. "I'm sure it is. Sloan

thinks highly of you…So, I think it will be a good fit… Anyway, why don't you take the rest of the day off. I have to go over some things with Agatha before I head home."

I walked out of Mr. Jenkins' office with a new outlook on things. I had a new promotion in the bag. I passed by Agatha. We shared a smile. I was sure Mr. Jenkins would fill her in.

Outside, the grin on my face only got bigger with each step I took towards the subway. A train was arriving when I made it to the platform. I got on and found a seat in the middle. As the doors closed, I felt myself dozing off, my thoughts on a crying horse.

Poems

The Beauty of Silence

The beauty of silence lies
within the noise.
the static within the air,
the ideas in your head,
the subtle emersion
into a world only you have access to.

Once School Has Finished

Neanderthal thinking,
crawling on all fours.
Extinct conceptual meanings,
the want and need through the lens of tears.
Leveled playing field, not counting home-runs.
Inclined grape-juice drinkers,
pouches in hand like sheets of classical music
waving in the heat.
This is a symphony.

Small white canines emerge.
Bright smiles color the beige walls with light.
Babies take flight down the drapes
of white silken sheets.
Joyful joy ride through the silence.
Fits by the minute–
salt pouring from pupils.
Hushing down by the faintest touch or candy.
The June days and Fall-Summer nights
have been wed.
Once school has finished.

A Dive Into the Deep End

I circled the pool,
eyed the water in it's calmest state,
looked for an opening.
I thought of the film scenes of cannon-balling,
the thousands of pool dives I witnessed.
And so I jumped.

I felt this bleached sea all around me,
And inside of me.
My nostrils, my ears, my eyes,
my whole body was consumed.
I was sinking lower and deeper.
When I looked to my right, I saw what I'd dived into:
The deep end.

On Walking to City Buildings

The legs walking by.
The job market expunged.
Railroads that get boarded.
The heels that click.
And the coffee that's brewed.

The elevator shafts.
The security footage captured.
The jackhammers punishing the pavement.
The gyro stand and the man with the cane,
I can't help but love it all.

Raffle Ticket Ponzi Scheme

A day long raffle.
Five prizes.
Famous teachers,
along with their manipulating institutions.
Orange tickets, two dollars a pop.
More tickets, more opportunity;
more kids, more unity.
A money laundering scheme really.

The funds go straight to the principal's box.
If not a principal's box, a church pew.
If not a church pew, a bootleg movie night.
If not a movie night, some desks and a party.
The real funds pay for the BMW's
and nights of wine and coke.
What a great progress and democracy,
this raffle ticket ponzi scheme.

Wooden Flakes of Fame

Appearances at the MET,
performances at the Y.
Tedx Talks,'
Loyal Backup band.
Simple chords and tunes,
movies and car tunes.
Wooden flakes of fame.

El Dorado lane,
band splits at the sinker.
Tour bus to the west,
eastern fanbase cremated.
Hard bottom boots and cayotes cackling.
Wooden flakes of fame.

Big venues,
vast scenerys.
Countrymen cookies,
and frontier beans.
Rider boots,
and writing teams.
Trip back to New York,
broadcasted on TV,
Big, wooden chunk of fame.

The Escape

The Faint sound of a mere crackle,
was all it took for one sabbatical.
The eerie foot movement
that plagued the minds of many
couldn't be ignored for a bag of pennies.
The Dungeon Now Opened.
Time elapsed,
passed along with the knapsack.
Chicken and anything else
thrown together.
The perfect getaway.

Summarizing lines of a script
felt like tips of charcoaled news clips.
The temperature now 70 degrees.
Black pavement hand warmth,
Ice cream lay melting away,
white shoe polish left in dismay.
The shell collapsed in his hand,
as the small man came into the shot.
Shadowed boom mikes with no inhabitants
Cut! Print!
An emotionless crowd left in amazement
by the filming of live a escape.

Cookies and Cashews

Cookies and cashews.
That's all it took.
Walnuts and cupcakes, maybe.
Gummy Bears and toothpicks possibly
Fruit Rollups or burnt strips of turkey bacon
probably
But five years down the drain over cookies
and cashews?
Really?

Subway Melting Pot

Meaningless carts,
meaningless thoughts.
Black floors,
silver poles.
Rusty old red seats,
dingy directions,
dirty maps,
Rhythmic trip to the city.

One adult, two babies—
3 and 4 aged kids,
Cart doors swinging ajar.
Loud speaker news,
windy stations,
Juicy gum chewing,
South ferry bound.

Bluetooths, ipods,
tunes, books, and newspapers.
Nike swoosh and blue jeans.
Tracksuits and gold chains.
Backpacks and donuts.
Hoodies and coffee.
Wall Streeters and bike couriers.
The big apple's diversity.

Minutes, Hours, Years

Seconds turn into minutes,
Minutes turn into hours,
Hours turn into days,
Days turn into weeks,
Weeks turn into months,
Months turn into years,
Years turn into eternity,
And some of ya'll just here
waiting for time to pass.

Crimson Train

White fangs, Halloween games.
The story of two teens
who went all out for a little fun.
It started in a basement.
Hard times when you're the cellar folk,
low and no where on anyone's social calendar.

But on this Halloween night, fate stepped in.
Or perhaps it was a routine coincidence.
The opportunity to befriend
Mr. Sampson, and his set of tools.

Teens just want to have fun on this night.
But these kids were deranged—
out looking for a victim
and some kind of change.
Bought themselves a war,
and brought along Mr. Sampson's chainsaw,
blending in among the many faux weapons
on this phony night.
Tracking down trick-or-treaters,
destined to be frozen in picture frames.
A cheerleader fell first.
The color of her skin faded
by a Crimson Train.

Been Waiting on This Day

Since I was three years old.
Thought about it.
Laughed about it.
Wrote about it.
Talked about it.
Vented about doing it.
Went about it.
Studied for it,
Now, I'm here.
I'm done.
One up, one down…

Deception

A true fabrication
The diction of a liar only out to win.
Morals up for grabs
and virtue in the distance
Doubt that will ever change—
courage and pride is something
that's in your veins.

They who appear as all things
they are not.
Residing and roaming at once;
diggers scratching at faith
with slippery hands.
No interest in knowledge.
Just a false sense of things
wound up in a ball of demise.

Tackle at the Picnic

Lilies and green grass,
wooden classy sandals,
peachy white dress,
white colored toes and fingernails,
brown skin,
full lips,
small pudgy nose,
hazel eyed beauty,
with the smile of a black-German daughter.

Green Grass.
Lilies in the field.
Wide open Terrain.
Air Max 2010 Games.
Camouflage cargos,
white tee,
navy blue Yankees fitted.
Smiles within,
glistening in the sunshine,
reflecting on the Benz

One leg up, second leg, too.
Churning chase sequence.
Slow motion sneakers.
Tackle of the century
into the enormous garden field.
A propped up Lillie stuck in her hair.
She laughed, then kissed me.

Bison Street

Night shift paper hikes.
Mill churning wills of power.
Speech refined, cold cuts resting.
Financial gains, opposing shops closed up.
Missing pages fluttering
from heavy gale winds.
The cold spine tingling,
a funeral home yards way.

6th Period

Infatuated girls
and little known drama.
Llama like postures of Greek mobsters,
King's and deputies.
Ritual rulers with tiger vests,
schoolyard prestigious crest
pummeled into a web of thread.
Eggheads and footballers,
Weeping queens and dunces.
Fondest memories of playtime incapacitated.

Middle school blues,
bellyaching fools.
Descriptive course classes
without concrete knowledge,
pathological lies, missing truths.
Egotistical teens,
arrogant teachers,
cocky model types and jocks.
As 6th period comes to an end,
you can see through the telescope
the future that will remain.

All Along the Lighthouse

Shards of remains lay hidden beneath the sand.
Liquor bottles sleeping in the sea.
Seashells crawling ashore.
Dolls and broken-handed Pails taking dirt naps.
And I found a dirty old ten dollar bill,
all along the lighthouse.

Rusty Arch

Enhanced discussion–
bass and percussion.
Times and lines.
Wall Street and China Town.
More music than fine art.
The clouds and wind.
Driving through the deep end of rush hour.
Coasting, arm on the holster.
Underneath us, I hear the roar
of the quiet stares
on the New York rail.

This is all B-Roll footage.
Stories rolling through my eyes.
Across the way I see Rusty Arch's brother,
as we leave Manhattan.
Then, we hit Rusty Arch.
and pop and I keep building.

Those Summertime Sprinklers

I miss those sprinklers.
When life was simpler.
When fun was a day in the street,
crashing through fire hydrant waterfalls.
When you could cup water in your hands,
and throw it at your friends.

I miss getting dressed for the sprinklers,
as if I was going to the pool.
Changing into swimming trunks,
wearing a white t-shirt and sandals.
I miss the walk up, then the race
to those summertime sprinklers.

Abu Amir

Crossword puzzles and Rap,
Then hustlin' back.
Superchamp Rounds,
and crowning the king of the match.
Pieces of tape on the floor,
helping my form.
Fashioning me into a machine,
Taking me to practice and criss-crossing
through the city with me.
Taking trips I grew up to need.
Pursuing the right opportunities.
The windows opened by basketball,
A facet of my repertoire necessary to my childhood.
Facilitating a learning experience
through a sport I loved.
Every time I walk through the front,
I think of all the games we had,
I still look forward to a new rim
at our new pad.

At 4, you continued to instill great things in me.
From writing to boxing,
bike riding and racecar driving.
I sat at my blue and grey table writing.
Crayons in disarray,
I only wanted to show you the color ice.

All the essays in grammar school,
helped me gain confidence and more interest;
gave me the will to write brand new sentences.
Printed out drafts that you helped me fix up.

Junior high came along
and you used my writing as acupuncture.
Thank you for the nights and mornings we stayed up.
Taught me discipline and routine.

Giving you "power" after pivotal discussions.
Writing for my occupation and future.
I would look at your face
and see a smile that meant a lot.
Helping me keep pushing to make myself better.
Writing made me happy,
and you knew it before I did.

Maybe Someday

You'll find me...
I won't make it hard for you.
I'll leave a track.
So maybe someday we could run into each other.
Maybe we'll spend another night together,
Or I'll say what I wanted to this time.

Maybe I'll remember.
Maybe I could explain.
I'll make you laugh again.
And we could get past it.
Maybe you'll understand.
Maybe someday we could bring
the family back together again.

Being on a Film Set

Being on a film set is like standing in a world
of espionage and war.
There are private eyes, henchmen,
heroes, and navigators.
The private eyes take you from basecamp.
The henchmen devour the craft services—
which are always stuffed with candy-store delights
and catered exclusives.
The navigators set up the shots.
The heroes jump into action,
that is, when the action is needed.

Then you have the pilots,
the conquistadors, the soldiers,
and the Vikings.
The pilots come up with the material.
The conquistadors make sure it's right.
The soldiers operate the equipment,
most often in stealth movements.
and the Vikings mark the spots for loot.

Then you have the astronomers.
The astronomers adjust the light.
And you have the scouts.
The scouts find the places
that make up the exteriors
of this special world.
Then there's the general,
who oversees the whole operation.
Then, on occasion, you have me,
the specialist—the doer and the observer;
the pilot and the Viking;
the astronomer and the scout;
the General and the soldier.

Round One

You meet a girl,
so the story goes.
You befriend her.
You want her, in secret.
You aim for an advantage.
You try to be smooth,
but you fuck it up;
and things get awkward.
But when you get back up
from off the mat,
you notice something:
She wants you, too.

Estranged

I hate it too.
The loneliness,
and not knowing.
The guilt that pours through.
The thoughts that roam.
The times I didn't listen,
Or the places I wouldn't go.

When you'd tell Pop that it wasn't my fault,
and I was the youngest, so I didn't deserve it anyway.
When you took the rap for me, no matter what.
And that time you told me
I was your partner in crime.
Or that night when you said
I could come to the movies.
These moments are fading echoes.

Because now, I don't know where you are,
who you stayed with.
What happened after college,
or what happened with Lydia.
All I have is a postcard in my hand
and a note that reads:
Be back later.

In the Batter's Box

Electrified intensity.
The triangle's been crossed twice;
it only gets dirtier.
Inching off the bag,
my teammates await to advance.
The stitching glides through the wind,
a glimmer of light shines off the Easton logo
on my bat.
Vocal box's go to sleep,
to be awakened by my swing.

Everybody Thinks the Same

Microwaved thoughts,
simple minded two faces.
Bandwagon-hoppers all out for a quick ride to the mix.
Standing on all two's.
Phonies, flawed clicks and other fake locals.
No one left to like.
Everybody thinks the same.

Waiting for the Waitress to Return

I had an epiphany,
cataclysmic mysteries stretched
beyond my modest memories
of her rhythmic heart beat.
I began to realize I missed her.
This feeling wasn't foreign;
my mind moved from one to another.
Sometimes my heart strayed
and laid back from all the confusion.
Although there was no love, yet,
there was a liking.

The way she took in the transaction
made the whole experience full of action.
She was the true contemporary art.
I watched her walk from our table,
back to the food, chefs, and dishwashers.
Where all the stock laid in disarray.
While she was gone, I received a kiss.
But I barely noticed.
I was waiting for the waitress to return.

Somewhere Between Here and There

It's like I'm in neutral
with nowhere to go.
As if I no longer have a purpose.
Like I'm just floating.
Don't know what it is,
or what I'm suppose to say.
Just know I'm lost,
and I've got to find my way back there.

American News on the TV

Hemorrhaging journalistic Abilities.
Crime and dumb downed cycles
Mummified citizens operating with breaking news
Break in;
a robbery;
vicious animal on the loose.
Fear as a joke—
"news" as a bully pulp figure's mantra.
T.V. on, same cycle.
Bickering, name calling.
Short interviews,
beat reporters paying dues,
and moron producers on the inside
shaping the news.

The School Hustle

Specialized tests,
English texts,
popular sects,
computer techs,
SAT Prep.
Juke right,
Juke left,
CAT Test.

Basement education.
Collegiate exploitation.
Great Expectations,
Dickens, Fitzgerald, nomenclature.
Excelling patience.
Syllabus blues.

Yellow trails of school,
noted fools.
Golden vests and pools.
Padded stats and spools,
I'm outta hear
in search of the truth's.

The Navy Blue Boat and the Stowaway

There was a boat.
A blue boat,
with a propeller attached to it's rear.
There was a hull, a sturdy hull,
with a hard shell.
There was a cabin with electronics,
and all you could eat.
And this boat,
this particular navy blue boat,
went out to sea.

Inside this boat,
this navy blue boat,
there was a stowaway—
an ex naval captain,
drunk of old age and whiskey.
He stumbled through
this blue boat mostly unseen,
and filled with fear.
The fear of never making it back to harbor.

Schoolyard Antics

Romancing amateur lovers.
Surprising French kisses.
Book bags dipped in gravel.
Monkey bar mansions.
Spanish dancing.
And the Schoolyard Police—
they spoil away the cool breezed spring shine;
the sugar rush of right foot/left foot churning.
No sympathy remains,
just symphonies of soon-to be awkward teens.

The Noble Narrator

Narrators who tell stories.
Pessimists who shoot em' down.
The voice of the speechless,
So-called minds of modern day geniuses.
Cutting pictures short.
Harder to live down a lack of ambition and execution.
Down in the dumps and dreams gone missing,
The narrator has the power
to pick you back up
and make you glisten.

Fat Brown

Tree limbs and dim streetlights,
rectangular shaped trunk and
oval shaped lamplight.
Fat brown and nine feet tall.
Brothers in arms.
The downfall of a lifetime,
climbing for centuries
to be the ultimate playground
and shade for parked cars.

The Middle's Arc

I feel it in my stomach.
My arms and legs.
Inside of my face.
Hovering in my mind.
Through my nose and ears.
I feel the cold chill seeping into my pores.

Numb to it all–
the people, I mean.
The expectations and the let downs.
The screaming and the yelling.
The bickering and the pressure.
The reminders of what could've been.
The doubts like raindrops walking on the future
And the worries of the past.
I'm past it all and comfortable in the middle's arc.

Stupid Diamond Smuglers

Volcano eruption.
Reliable nothing's.
The counter plan.
Hourly refined airplane modules.
Transferred pesos.
Ticketing Centers.
Previous tests, chumps aside.
New faces and chest full of diamonds

Satin blue napkins
Wristwatch glistening.
New shipment on its way.
Jetting through carpools and 80s Dudes'
Paranoid progress.
Two Dutchmen and a lockness
ready to rush in and tackle,
Bag, then handcuff.

Brooklyn's Finest Girls, Part 1

Pretty girls come from everywhere.
In Bushwick,
where the rice and beans flow,
and the elevated trains plow through.
In Crown Heights,
where the dollar vans race for customers,
and the Jamaican eateries deal out patties.
In Flatbush,
where the West Indians parade and party,
and the bake-scented blocks go for unending miles.
In East New York,
where the basketball tournaments are jumpin,'
and the cookouts bleed into the next morning.
In Park Slope,
where the café's and ice cream shops scatter about,
and the kids run wild.

In a Room

In a room full of morons,
how do I stand out?
In a room full of idiots,
how can I lead?
In a room full of ignorance,
how can I breath?
In a room full of chatter,
how can I speak?
Fuck it.
I'll just leave and capture some peace.

Knuckles

My knuckles have been through
Brick and cobble road,
grass and dirt,
jaws, chalkboards,
and chest bones.
But there was a time when
my knuckles couldn't get through.

Under Review

Fans roaring,
bright lights,
arena rocking.
Three point deficit,
brand new 24.
Lob pass to the point,
dished away for a score.
Timeout.
Tie game,
Knotted up at 98.

Arena music blasting.
Slushies spilling.
Tensions brewing.
Coaches sweating,
players breathing heavy.

The refs review the three.
It's a two pointer.
The game's over.

At the Workplace Watching Time Go By

Clocks everywhere,
raised by flying times.
Hours like weapons,
slithery connections.
Minutes and pistols,
bullets as seconds.
Unknown targets in the range.

Hidden American pastimes.
Reams of paper soldiers
sit at grey tables,
haunted by color.
The clocks are everywhere,
reminding them that time is running out.

Performance Day

Laced up flats and black leggings.
Heads Turning and legs flexing.
Broken necks, sliding From side to side.
Air gliding, eerily distant eyes
landing on every moment.
Laid over on-lookers.
Bright faces, glistening and gleaming.
Happy teachers, table of peaches.
One toss and whirl by,
airborne with no alibi.
Bumpy landing, the becoming of failure.

Deep panic, followed by sadness,
befallen inner parts
Frowns with no upside down magic.
Scholarship trashed;
confidence confiscated.
New arrangements with litigations.
Training faded with the dull cadence
of ambitious rain skin
Saving face covered in tears of pride.
Her performance day ruined.

Cement, Won't You Turn Gray Again?

Black spots from commuters.
Gum drops and Snapple tops,
blue bags and blue magic,
Lays chips and soda.
Cement, won't you turn gray again?

Skid marks from baby strollers.
Plastic supermarket bags
gliding along.
Pieces of shattered liquor bottles
and old crushed beer cans.
Cracks all across your back.
Cement, won't you turn gray again?

Tattoos

Foster care and lonesome.
Home alone with no one.
Rough pillows and thin sheets.
dirty socks and dirty feet.
Left-over lumpy milk
with expired Cheerios.
Ripped clothes, but not as fashion.
The struggle.

Battered memories:
A crushed voice box.
Salty eyes and fading futures;
stained skin and crusty nails.
Pale pigments and frail bodies,
damaged hair and dry scalps.
Bird chests and white mouths.
All tattoos of her hardened life.

Film Criticism

Rope, Hitchcock's 10-Shot Masterpiece

December 31, 2010 (age 14)

Perhaps one of the scariest, creepiest films I've ever seen is *Rope* (1948). Mind you, this film isn't supposed to be a horror flick. In fact, it's a crime inspired by real life events—the 1924 murder of Bobby Franks by two University of Chicago students, Leopold and Loeb.

Rope is about two friends who set out to commit the "perfect crime". Brandon Shaw (John Dall) and Phillip Morgan (Farley Granger) share an apartment in New York. They feel high and mighty, and certainly much more superior than David Kentley (Dick Hogan), their friend from school. Brandon and Phillip plan what they think to be the perfect murder. And after killing David and hiding his body in their apartment, they decide to invite their friends over for a party. What else?

Presumably testing out their theory of a "perfect crime," Brandon, the leader, toys with his visitors, in particular, a former teacher, Rupert Cadell (James Stewart). Wrong move, as things unravel when Rupert figures out that David is dead, and that Brandon and Phillip killed him.

Making a film inspired by real life events is always a daunting task. But in the especially heinous case of Leopold and Loeb, it must have been even more difficult for director Alfred Hitchcock (even with the guidance of Patrick Hamilton's 1929 play). Nevertheless, for a number of reasons, Hitchcock's *Rope*, is a flawless piece of filmwork that captured the nature and essence of the story.

Alfred Hitchcock only used ten shots the entire film! This means he had to use a series of long shots in the film. In fact, the way in which the shots were streamed (cut) and put together make the film appear to be one long continuous shot. The first time I saw *Rope*, I thought what I was seeing was the work of the editor. But, in effect, there wasn't much editing going on in the film. Instead, the way in which Hitchcok utilized just ten shots made the entire film seamless.

But this was revolutionary, because at that time such an aesthetic strategy was unheard of. I think that the film's ten shots worked effectively, and must have taken a lot of planning and rehearsal to execute. I'd like to know how much film was used going with this technique, and how they had everything set up and reading to keep shooting without any glitches.

I should also mention that the entire cast did a wonderful job of staying within themselves during the long scenes. On screen, it moved with the pacing of a live play.

The camera shots and elongated acting in *Rope* changed my view of how films could be arranged and shot. The simple, but carefully organized cinematography in *Rope* blew me away. Again, using only ten shots in an 80 minute film is certainly not an easy task. But Hitchcock and his crew made it look easy, and changed film forever.

And it wasn't like these were new shots or anything. The shots utilized in the film were all prototype. What I mean is, they were shots that everybody had seen before. For example, close-ups, reaction shots, and extreme close-ups, had long been in use. But the manner, fashion, and time of the shots is what revolutionized film, creating a new way to structure a film.

Collateral, A Great Twist on the Hitman Narrative

March 14, 2011 (Age 15)

In *Collateral* (2004), a Los Angeles cab driver named Max (Jamie Foxx) is forced to become the getaway driver for a hitman named Vincent (Tom Cruise). Soon, Max has two decisions to make: How to save himself and Vincent's last target.

The hitman narrative has been recycled for years. But director Michael Mann takes it up a notch with the innovative cab driver/get-away-driver narrative device. I've never seen a hit man flick use the vehicle, literally and figuratively, and a cab driver to move the story along.

Another feature that stands out in Collateral is the frenemy relationship that's established between Max and Vincent. Jamie Foxx and Tom Cruise are both very skilled actors, and in *Collateral* each delivers one of their best performances thus far. To say the least, Foxx and Cruise's chemistry powers what has to be the thing that keeps the movie together. And while each seems to rub off on the other, it's Max who seems to benefit the most. By the end of the film, Max, a big talker and somewhat of a coward, finds boldness and courage inside himself.

What I also liked about *Collateral*, which was shot on digital, was the editing. Editors Jim Miller and Paul Rubell did a great job; in fact, they were nominated for an Academy Award for Best Editing for *Collateral.* I'm not surprised. *Collateral* featured a tight, clean editing strategy. Througout the film, you feel the presence of well thought out and planned editing. I don't know if this is the usual when a team of two editors work together, but I wonder exactly how they do it. Like who's responsible for what?

Editing and cinematography always goes hand in hand in my book. And in *Collateral*, the cinematography adds another layer of looming doom. Like when Vincent pulls his first hit, and the victim is thrown from an apartment window and dropped on the hood of Max's cab. I thought that scene was shot and cut exceptionally well; the hood of the cab virtually exploded!

Collateral did fairly well at the box office. It was liked by many critics but not loved by most. However, to me it's a four star film, all things considered.

The 'Burbs, a Somewhat Elaborate Comedy that Shines Nonetheless

October 26, 2010 (age 14)

The 'Burbs (1989) is about a suburbanite, Ray Peterson (Tom Hanks) and his neighbors, Art Weingartner (Rick Ducommun) and Lt. Mark Rumsfield (Bruce Dern), who struggle to prove that the new family (the Klopeks) in town is a group of cannibals. During the adventure, Ray and Art go to desperate measures, even sneaking into the Klopeks' house while they're away. Of course, nobody believes Ray and Art, that is until they're finally able to get proof, and avoid prison time.

The 'Burbs, directed by Joe Dante, has a decent storyline that's often funny. Ray's the sanity of the whole operation, while Art's the conspiracy theory nut. And these two characters make for great comedy.

I was surprisingly impressed with the camera angles used in *The 'Burbs.* It's an ordinary comedy, nothing spectacular, so you wouldn't expect elaborate camera angles. However, it puts new spins on classic comedic camera angles, like the rapid zoom in and zoom out shot on the character's screaming or laughing. Also, your standard extreme close up on frightened characters. Cinematography also helped with the scenes including the Klopeks. Plus, the night scenes used a lot of street lights, and special effects.

While *The 'Burbs* won't garner best pic vote from most people, it is a solid film. The film was much better than I expected. I thought it would be heavy on the slapstick, but it wasn't. The storyline was developed well; and the chemistry between the main characters allowed subtle jokes to go over naturally. I felt the film exhibited what a comedy should be. For that, I give *The 'Burb's* three stars.

A Trio of Sisters Find Three Different Ways Out of '50s Harlem Ghetto in *Sparkle*

October 19, 2010 (age 14)

Sparkle (1976) is, to this day, one of my favorite films. The first time that I saw it, I couldn't have been no more than 5 or 6. Now that I'm older, it still holds up. When I was younger, I couldn't grasp some of the events and references that take place in the film. But I didn't care, I liked the film anyway. *Sparkle*, directed by Sam O'Steen, isn't a film you just watch for entertainment, there's a lot that goes on. This film hits you hard in the gut.

Sparkle is about three singing sisters, Sister (Lonette McKee), Delores (Dwan Smith), and Sparkle (Irene Cara) from Harlem who dream of making it big and getting out the Harlem ghetto. Each sister takes an entirely different path, and it isn't always pretty. However, they do try to stick together, and I liked that about the story. Unfortunately, tragedy strikes, and the once very close sisters are forced apart. *Sparkle* is at times happy, but the despair and sadness never really leaves.

Sparkle's storyline is not a necessarily unfamiliar one, but what I really liked is how you could feel each individual story behind each character. I was able to connect with everyone in the film, and I felt exactly the way all of the story arcs were intended to make me feel.

Another aspect of *Sparkle* that I liked was the lighting. Lighting was natural (at times pretty dark), and it played a key role in a number of scenes. For example, the first time the sisters sang together, the lighting helped show the natural "star light" of Sister, the oldest and most adventureous of the three. Another scene in which I was struck by the lighting that was used in a backstage scene was the dressing room lights were the only source of light.

I give *Sparkle* four stars, and not because it's one of my favorite films, but because the acting, storyline, editing, lighting, and direction is all first rate.

Tarantino's Stripped Down *Reservoir Dogs* Makes for Gritty Heist Movie

March 1, 2011 (age 14)

Reservoir Dogs (1992) is about a very well-planned jewel heist that goes horribly wrong because one of the thieves in the crew is really an undercover cop. In this psychological, bare bones heist genre film, Tarantino gives the familar undercover cop narrative a new twist, using the natural cause and effect of a such a situation to create a running conflict and many memorable scenes.

After being shot, one of the members of the crew, who as it turns out is the cop, is brought back to the meeting place. In true Tarantino, non-linear story-telling fashion, we learn early on who the cop is and how he lands a spot in the crew. Along the way, we're also given a close up of how the big caper was put together by old school crime boss Joe Cabot (Lawrence Tierney) and his son, "Nice Guy" Eddie (Chris Penn).

Each guy in the crew, mostly strangers to each other, is given a false name, a color actually. There's Mr. White (Harvey Keitel), Mr. Blonde (Michael Madsen), Mr. Orange (Tim Roth), Mr. Pink (Steve Buscemi), Mr. Blue (Eddie Bunker), and Mr. Brown (Quentin Tarantino).

The storyline itself is really straight forward and rather simple. But Tarantino's non-linear approach to storytelling opens up the otherwise simple story into something complicated and irresistible to watch.

I also really liked Tarantino's use of colors for the names of the guys in the crew (e.g. Mr. Blonde, Mr. White, Mr. Pink). I think that was a simple but clever idea, not only because it satisfied the need for cool names in a genre film like this, but because it added a touch of humor, which helped make each character in the crew even more sinister.

One thing about this film that I really like is how it's edited. *Reservoir Dogs* uses a lot of different kinds of cuts and edits that include frames with multiple characters. What I mean is, sometimes it may seem like a montage is at work, but it's just the way the film is edited with different scenes. For example, in the opening scene a series of wheel shots are strung together with the point of views of all the main characters.

The lighting is another aspect of the film that stood out for me. Ever since I started paying attention to lighting in the films that I watch, I've found natural light usually to be the most effective in getting great visuals. Still, *Reservoir Dogs* had to rely on artificial lighting for much of the film. Most of the story unfolds within a small warehouse. There was little time I devoted to the actual heist itself. But the foot-chase scene had great natural lighting that helped it look realistic.

Reservoir Dogs is a four star film. The direction, storyline, editing, cinematography and lighting combined to make for a great film. I'm a fan of Tarantino's films, and *Reservoir Dogs* is my 3rd favorite, behind *Kill Bill* (I & II) and *Pulp Fiction.*

Zombieland, Horror Spoof Done Right

April 11, 2011 (age 15)

Since *Zombieland* (2009) came out in theaters last year, I wanted to see it, but I didn't get to catch it before it left. So while at home one day, I had just finished watching *Adventureland* on cable on the Starz channel. After the movie ended, there was a promo for the premier of *Zombieland;* it was going to air in a couple of weeks. So I committed that date to memory, and planned to watch it. But it was to no avail. Something came up. Then I placed *Zombieland* in my Netflix instant queue, but I passed over it numerous times. But Thursday morning, I finally caught *Zombieland* on one of the Starz channels. Here's a breakdown of the film.

In a world full of zombies that have spread across America, four people find each other and try to survive. Columbus (Jesse Eisenberg) who's survived by following his "thirty rules", finds Tallahassee (Woody Harrelson) in Columbus, Ohio. Once the two get together, they decide to head to Florida. Along the way, they run into two girls, including one who appears to be bitten by a zombie. However, Wichita (Emma Stone) and Little Rock (Abigail Breslin) aren't as helpless as they look. After a couple thefts here and there, the four realize they're all the family they've got in *Zombieland.* (Note—I thought it was cool how all of the characters were named after their home city.)

The storyline of *Zombieland* is a hopeless one, but the comidic twist makes this movie for me. Had the film been a gory horror picture, I don't think anything in Zombieland would've worked; it would've just been your run-of-the-mill zombie movie. And although I liked the storyline, I think a couple of scenes could've been developed some more to give a better explanation of each character's background.

Editing was key in *Zombieland.* Not only was the film a

comedy, it was also a horror film, and it had to portray this. The editing in the film was rather quick during the zombie chasing scenes, and rightfully so. In the scenes where we get context on the characters, the editing was slow but with a hint of hurried energy. The characters always had some where to be, but they still had enough time to find out about each other, and I think that's where the editing was most effective.

Far as the camera angles and lighting, *Zombieland* used a couple clever techniques. For example, whenever Columbus spoke of one of his rules, there would usually be sub-titles of the rule that summarized everything he had to say. Most of the time he spoke of one of his rules there would be a wide shot that took up Columbus and the rule that appeared near his shoulder. I thought that was clever. Lighting was useful because most of the film was shot during the day, so I think a lot of natural light was used. Of course, the night scenes had to use artificial lighting.

The acting in *Zombieland* was decent. Jesse Eisenberg as Columbus was great casting. In fact, casting was good across the board. None of the actors tried to overplay their roles, or outshine the next. But clearly because of the structure of the storyline, Jesse Eisenberg was the star, and everyone else was support. Still, the chemistry between the actors was good.

After watching *Zombieland*, I told my father I thought the film was a solid two stars. But now, having thought about it more deeply, I think the film should get a boost—two and a half stars. Some aspects of the film make it three stars. But there are also some aspects that make it a one and a half-star flick. But I liked all of the characters. I think a lot can be learned from this film, especially for those who dig the spoof genre.

Lock, Stock, and Two Smoking Barrels, Quintessential Modern British Crime Drama with Genius Parallel Stories

April 3, 2011 (age 15)

Lock, Stock, and Two Smoking Barrels (1998) tells the story of four friends Eddy (Nick Moran), Tom (Jason Flemyng), Bacon (Jason Statham), and Soap (Dexter Fletcher), who get caught up on the wrong side of London ganster named Harry "Harry the Hatchet" Lonsdale. After the guys pool together the required buy-in money for Harry's private big-money card game, Eddy, the skilled card player of the bunch, is cheated out of the buy-in, plus an additional 400,000 pounds that is loaned to him at the table by none other than Harry himself. Now, 500,000 pounds in debt to Harry, the guys have just one week to pay Harry back, or else.

I'll tell you what, in a situation like this, some kind of heist is inevitable. There's just few other ways to get that kind of money in such little time. And heist is exactly what happens. But it's not your ordinary heist!

Director Guy Ritchie did a great job of managing and executing multiple layers of the storyline. I was in awe by how well he was able to pull it off. I think it's partly because of the British crime film style of dialogue and detail. But when you consider that *Lock, Stock, and Two Smoking Barrels* has multiple parallel stories running throughout the film, you just have to tip your hat to Ritchie (who's style has drawn comparison with American filmmaker Quentin Tarantino).

Editing is fundamentally important to any film, but it's absolutely essential when narrating parallel storylines and various sub-narratives. And in *Lock, Stock, and Two Smoking Barels,* the editing works a great silent narrator. For example, in the scenes involving a small outfit of marijuana growers, who as it turns out, work for another London gangster named Rory Breaker (Vas Blackwood), the editing helps to keep you well-orientated to how the heist part of the story unravels.

The lighting in *Lock, Stock, and Two Smoking Barrels* gives the film a gritty and worn look and feel. I also liked the cinematography. Although the film's shot well throughout, I thought the best shots were found towards the end and middle of the film. Still, I really liked how the crooked card game was shot in the beginning of the film. There were multiple shots of each player's reaction and the angles seemed like you were on a merry-go-round. Towards the end of the film, the shots were mostly of action and quick reactions, as you would expect from violent climax scenes.

Lock, Stock, and Two Smoking Barrels launched the careers of Jason Statham, and former International footballer turned actor, Vinnie Jones. While Statham was pretty much a semi-critical character in the film, Jason Flemyng was the leader of the friends, Vinnie Jones' enforcer character was brilliant.

Lock, Stock and Two Smoking Barrels is less known and underrated here in America. And that's not surprising; this isn't a film for everyone. But I'm a big crime drama fan. Plus, as far as directing, writing, acting, editing, lighting, and cinematography goes this is one of the most exceptional films I've seen yet. Needless to say, *Lock, Stock and Two Smoking Barrels* gets four stars.

Attack of *The Birds*

December 8, 2010 (age 14)

Perhaps the first "horror" film that I completely grasped was *The Birds* (1963) directed by Alfred Hitchcock. Growing up, I watched *The Birds* a lot—I mean multiple times a day! (I first started watching it when I was 3 years old.)

The story begins when Melanie Daniels (Tippi Hedren), a rich upper-class woman, meets Mitch Brenner (Rod Taylor) in a pet shop one day. Mitch pulls a prank on Melanie ,which she doesn't take too kindly. To repay Mitch, she follows him. Where the two spend the weekend is where the otherwise love story takes a crazy turn...for the worst, as wild birds go bat-shit and attack every human in sight.

The Birds has a very simple yet effective storyline. In it's essence, the film is about a flock of birds that go berzerk on a number of humans one weekend in San Francisco. The fact that there's a parallel love story almost doesn't even matter, because the terror of the birds is so menacing. Plus, a "horror" film with a strong romantic connection between two absolute strangers? I suppose that's how it goes when you've only got one person to protect you.

The camera shots and angles used in *The Birds* took the film to another level. The attack scenes were violent, sad and scary all in one, and camera angles played this up. Like when Melanie was directly attacked by a group of birds, each taking its own peck on her. In this shot, the bird's eye view angle was so that you feel the birds pecking, leaving the you to wonder how much more pain and torture she could possibly take. And the worm's eye view angle showed the aftermath of the attack.

Tippi Hedren and Rod Taylor both delivered solid performances in their respective characters. Although, I've always had the feeling that this was one of those films where practically any male actor would have been useful. Mainly because I think Tippi Hedren's scenes really drove *The Birds*.

Editing was a solid component to *The Birds*, but with all the action and storyline development I didn't really notice it. I plan on seeing *The Birds* again to key in on the editing. I do wonder if editing played a big or minimal role in the film's ultimate success.

My guess is that the editing played a huge role in *The Birds*. But as with other Hitchcock films that I've studied, I've yet to crack exactly what editing approach he's taking.

The Birds will always be on my permanent favorite films list. The combination of direction, realistic action, cinematography, and believable acting make *The Birds* one of those movies not easy to forget. When I was 3 years old, I'm sure I didn't bother to rate *The Birds*; I just watched it everyday like it was a cartoon. But when I got older, and started closely watching it, I considered it to be a solid three and a half-star film.

Two Great Twists Make *Hancock* a Surprisingly Good Superhero Film

December 19, 2010 (age 14)

When I first saw the trailer for *Hancock* (2008), I figured that the film would be full of fluff. A big money superhero movie with nothing engaging to offer. I also thought that the film would be just a cliché superhero quickly thrown together by Hollywood, with Will Smith's name as the selling point. However, when I did get around to seeing the film—on cable, I was completely and happily surprised.

Hancock is about a lonely, down and out, once respected, alcoholic superhero, who can't be injured or killed, named Hancock (Will Smith), who gets an image makeover from a public relations executive named Ray (Jason Bateman). When Ray brings Hancock home to meet the family, Ray's wife Mary (Charlize Theron) appears to welcome Hancock into the family's home, even accepting Ray's PR idea. But after repeated trips to the home and increased time with Ray, Mary doesn't want the washed-up superhero anywhere near her family. Only thing is, Hancock is interested in Mary, but he doesn't know why. The two have a connection that Hancock can't figure out. But Mary knows.

In the midst of all this, Hancock still has a few problems to deal with. And when one of those problems finally catches up to him, catastrophe strikes, and Hancock is forced into action. However, this it's not only his life that is in jeopardy, but Mary's as well.

The storyline of Hancock has a couple of layers and twists that make it one of the best superhero films/love stories I've ever seen. As mentioned, there's the layer of the wash-up superhero who gets a new image. There's the PR guy who bets on a bum superhero. And there's Hancock's and Mary's mysterious connection. Each layer is woven together fantastically by director Peter Berg, and the story never sours, especially when we learn that Hancock is not the only superhero in the film.

There were so many great things that I didn't see it coing, it makes me wonder who was in charge of the initial marketing roll out of *Hancock*, because, they did not market this film right. But I suppose they didn't want to give away the main twist.

While I think the story (Vincent Gilligen and Vince Ngo) itself was the best part of the film, I also think there were some very strong performances by Will Smith, Charlize Theron, and Jason Bateman. In *Hancock,* Smith had the emotion and physicality down pat! I believed that he was an alcoholic superhero suffering from depression. I also believed that Charlize Theron was a loving housewife who didn't want Hancock to ruin her husband's career or their family. (The on-screen chemistry between her and Will Smith is superb!) And Jason Bateman was very convincing as a PR man with heart.

As I mentioned at the beginning, going before I saw *Hancock*, I expected it to be worthless. Instead, it was one of the most rewarding film screenings I've ever had. Aside from the fact that it has a great storyline, great acting, and the most stunning visuals we'll likely ever see of Charlize Theron, Hancock is, surprisingly, a real feel-good movie. I give it a solid three stars.

On the Waterfront, A Real Contender for the Perfect Film

December 25, 2010 (age 14)

On the Waterfront is about an ex-prize fighter turned longshoremen named Terry Malloy (Marlon Brando), who struggles to stand up against his "union" bosses. Terry was on his way to the top as a boxer. Then, after Terry's encouraged by his brother, Charley (Rod Steiger), to take the fall so some mob guy can make some money, his boxing career goes down the tank. But one saving grace: Terry and his brother had a spot with a crew that they could never shake. The only way to escape is by death, but Terry's not ready to go out. A film full of twists and turns, Terry ultimately accomplishes something in his life.

The storyline for *On the Waterfront* was realistic, and the writing was some of the finest I've seen played on screen. I found Terry's story to be both sad and inspirational. In fact, I suspect that anyone who watches *On the Waterfront* will connect with Terry on some level.

All around, the acting in this film was spectacular! Before I saw this movie, I had only seen Marlon Brando in *The Godfather.* Man, what a difference. Not that he wasn't good in *The Godfather*, just he must've been in his prime in *On the Waterfront.* Every scene he was in, he was brilliant and right on point. For example, the scene where Terry and Charley are taking a ride was great. Both Brando and Steiger were playing off of each other's energy and responses, and the scene felt authentic and heartfelt. Another scene that shows Brando at his best is the scene near the docks with Terry and Edie (Eva Marie Saint). Brando turned on the emotion in a way that pulls you right into the scene.

I'm a fan of black and white movies, particularly because of how the lighting was often used. *On The Waterfront* utilized a balance of natural and artificial light. But both techniques were equally effective. Natural light was used most effectively in the scenes were Brando was alone with his thoughts on the roofs of his home. Also, natural light was effective, especially so in the very last scene when Terry was having his last walk. And the artificial light that was used in all of the scenes with Johnny Friendly (Lee J. Cobb) and his henchmen made them look even more evil.

Having watched *On The Waterfront* for the first time, I came away with two conclusions. First, I know why *On The Waterfront* is considered one of the best films of all time. This film is virtually perfect. I didn't find one wrong element in the movie. Second, Marlon Brando is one of the best actors ever.

On The Waterfront gets four stars no question.

***Black Belt Jones*, 70s Karate Comedy—Albeit Unintentionally**

August 7, 2010 (age 14)

For some reason, *Black Belt Jones* (1974) was a film that I cherished as a kid. But when I got older, I decided to test my film knowledge and see if I still felt the same way. And anyway, I wanted to catch a 70s flick for my daily screening. So I went to my family's film shelf, and grabbed our VHS copy of *Black Belt Jones.*

Black Belt Jones is a 70s karate flick starring Jim Kelly as Black Belt Jones and Gloria Hendry as Sidney, his love interest. It's about an ex-karate master's (Sidney's father) karate studio being taken over by a hood, who works for the local mob. Black Belt Jones assembles a team to take down the mob before they can get hold of the karate studio.

When I was younger, I thoroughly enjoyed *Black Belt Jones.* I can remember eating lunch and watching every frame, and just cracking up. I thought the movie was hilarious. And I didn't really consider the storyline, or its structure, at all. But wow, at 14, I realize that what I was laughing at back then wasn't *supposed* to be funny—Black Belt Jones isn't a comedy!

To say the least, the storyline is flawed. In fact, it's confusing and, at times, ridiculous. I'm not sure if the director, Robert Clouse, misinterpreted the story in *Black Belt Jones*, or if he just didn't know what to make of such a poorly structured storyline. Either way, it seems clear to me that he had no idea which directon he wanted to go in. So he just decided to smash together comedy and drama. In my opinion, Cluse should've just made *Black Belt Jone*s a comedy, because that's really what worked the best in the film.

My rating for *Black Belt Jones* is 2 stars.

Ponyo, An Enduring Tale About a Young Boy and His Goldfish Friend

February 21, 2011 (age 15)

Hayao Miyazaki is a Japanese filmmaker known for animation. He's directed a number of films and has illustrated several Manga issues (comics and print cartoons). However, the first time I heard of director Hayao Miyazaki was last year one day when I was listening to an NPR segment on him. At the time, he had a film set for release in a couple weeks called *Ponyo* (2008). After hearing that his *Ponyo* would be shown at Symphony Space, I went to see it. Below is my review.

Ponyo is an animated feature about a 5-year old loner, Sosuke, who discovers a goldfish on the beach, and he names her *Ponyo*. Sosuke's father is a sailor and his mother works for a senior citizen home nearby. Because of their jobs, Sosuke is at home by himself a lot. But when he finds *Ponyo*, everything changes. *Ponyo* is no ordinary goldfish; she's the daughter of a powerful wizard and sea goddess. And as the story goes, *Ponyo* has powers that will change the world.

I liked Ponyo. I thought the storyline was solid, and I think it was executed well. It effectively used the theme of a lonely person who finds a magical friend. I could feel Sosuke's loneliness, and I understood that his only escape was his imagination. Of course, when Ponyo comes along, he gets a friend.

The editing in *Ponyo* was choppy and quick. The story and film didn't waste time at all, it got straight to the point. Thus, the editing followed. The only time the editing was jagged or slow was when a sinister or sad scene was on the horizon. The acting wasn't anything special since it was an animated film. That being said, I think the voice for Sosuke fit perfectly with the child's animated face.

Ponyo is a children's story with the range to touch adult hearts and minds. It's certainly one of the better animated films I've seen. At its root, it's a love story with a touch of "magical lands," and it includes a quest to be "human." For those reasons I give Ponyo a solid three stars.

Buster Keaton Stars in *The General*, A Silent Film Gem

March 22, 2011 (age 15)

Before screening *The General* I'd only seen three other silent films. But each one of them were shorts. So I had mixed feelings going in to see The General, as it would be the first full-length silent film that I screen. Here's my breakdown.

The General is about an engineer, Johnny (Buster Keaton), who tries to save his train, "The General," after the Union steals it. When the Civil War begins, Johnny is forced to enlist in the army. But his service is turned down (after numerous attempts) because he's better as an engineer. His wife, Annabelle (Marion Mack) refuses to speak to him until he's enlisted in the army. Then one day, "The General" is taken with Annabelle onboard, and Johnny is thrust into action.

A Storyline told through subtitles and action wasn't a new concept to me. Most foreign films with English subtitles used to be the same way to me. I've been watching foreign films with my father since I was 3 years old. And because I didn't quite understand everything, it might as well had been a silent film. Nonetheless, *The General's* storyline is structured very well. The storyline has a solid foundation that allows you to follow along easily.

I was surprised by the camera angles used in *The General.* Like the scene where Johnny is on a train that appears to be moving slowly down a railroad. The thing you notice is how incredibly wide the shot is, and how the shot seems to keep zooming in and out, showing Keaton's face and his inevitable fate. Most of the other shots in the film were used to give off huge amounts of slapstick laughter.

I think the editing in *The General* was pretty basic; nothing immediately stood out to me. Since this is a silent film, a lot of the edits are used to showcase the titles on black that describe the upcoming scenes. There were also some scenes that seemed to dissolve into one another, which I thought was effective in getting certain parts of the storyline across.

Silent films are a new form to me. And starting off with *The General*, a film considered to be one of the best films of all time, is a huge plus. The bonus is that I really liked the film. I give it three and a half stars.

It Happened One Night Hits All the Marks You'd Expect from a Screwball Comedy and Society Picture

January 17, 2012 (age 15)

For film review class we screened *It Happened One Night*. This film is one more film in a long line of screwball comedies that my class plans on screening. I've gotten accustomed to the new style of comedy that we've decided to delve into. I'm starting to notice things that aren't typical in a modern day comedy. For example, there isn't much comedy in this genre. It may be that to my peers and I we don't find certain things funny, but I can argue that's not the case, and that certain intended jokes are more serious. Nonetheless, here's a breakdown of *It Happened One Night*.

In *It Happened One Night* (1934) directed by Frank Capra, a recently engaged Ellie Andrews (Claudette Colbert) finds love and a new husband, Peter Warne (Clark Gable) on a bus headed to New York. Ellie happens to be an heiress who's trying to run away from her father to see her husband, "King" Westley (Jameson Thomas), whom her father doesn't approve of. Peter is out for a story after he loses his job as a writer for a newspaper in New York. As screwball comedies go, Ellie and Peter find each other in an odd way, then continue their unorthodox journey together.

It Happened One Night, at its roots, is a story about how love can be found in the most inopportune times and odd situations. But in *It Happened One Night*, this theme is also used to comment on the failure of arranged marriages. Another thing I noticed, something that I also found in *My Man Godfrey*—another screwball comedy/society picture—is how the male character is at least ten years older than the female character. I'm not sure what's this is supposed to mean, but I think that plays a role in the film. Plus, in both films, the girls were considered to be "spoiled brats," who were *set straight* by the men that they then fell in love with.

There were a number of things that I liked about *It Happened One Night.* But I especially liked how most of the scenes transitioned. Most of all the scenes dissolved to black and then appeared with action in the next scene. I like that editing technique and style. I think it's really effective, because when you dissolve to black and then have the action pick up after a black screen, it sort of builds up anticipation. Plus, it also gives viewers a brief moment to digest everything that has just happened.

I didn't find anything to be outstanding about the cinematography in *It Happened One Night.* Besides a couple wheel shots here and there, the film's camera angles were simple and straight forward. Lighting was an assortment of natural light, artificial, and smoke from cigarettes or an occasional pipe of course. But above all, I liked how a lot of street lights and car head lights were used as extra lighting sources in numerous scenes. For example, in the bus scene when Peter gets off and starts talking to Shapeley (Roscoe Karns), the bus headlights fueled that whole scene. Also, in the last scene, headlights and streetlights were both used to supply the action.

Overall, I liked *It Happened One Night a lot.* As far as screwball comedies/society pictures go, it had a good storyline and great acting of course. I also thought director Frank Capra did an excellent job of directing. Thus, my rating for *It Happened One Night* is three and a half-stars.

Ridiculed High School Loner Gets Revenge in *Carrie*, Brian De Palma's Hauntingly Good Adaptation of the Stephen King Novel

June 10, 2010 (age 14)

Whenever I watch *Carrie* (1976), I can never seem to catch it from the beginning. Whether *Carrie* will be on at 7:00pm, and I'm already sitting in front of my T.V. by 6:55, something will come up. Or if *Carrie* is due to air again at 9:00pm on another night, I'll be ready, my scheduled cleared and popcorn ready, but something will come up again. I've seen *Carrie* at least 15 times, but just bits and pieces. I've only seen *Carrie* straight through three times.

Carrie, directed by Brian De Palma and based on the Stephen King novel of the same name, is about an awkward, High School loner named Carrie (Sissy Spacek), who uses her special powers to get revenge at prom after being miserably embarrassed by the cool kids.

Sissy Spacek is great as Carrie, and her co-stars all carry their weight as well. Director Brian De Palma is in top form with all of his choices, but I particularly liked how he used lighting to make the scenes with Carrie even more horrifying.

Overall, *Carrie* is a good horror flick. It's not epic, and I like the book more. But as far as adaptions go, *Carrie* is first rate. I give it three stars—four stars if you count its classic appeal.

In *The Last Samurai*, Washed-Up Civil War Hero Gets Redemption in Japan

December 12, 2011 (age 15)

The Last Samurai (2003), directed by Edward Zwick, centers around a Civil War soldier named Nathan Algren (Tom Cruise), who is hired by an American middle-man to help train Japanese soldiers in the modern way of fighting and warfare. Nathan and his good friend Zebullon Gant (Billy Connolly) quickly train the new Japenese soldiers and prepare them for an attack against the Samaurai who refuse to give up their ancient tradition. When the attack goes horribly wrong, Nathan is captured, and the leader of the Samurai, Katsumoto (Ken Watanabe), spares his life because he showed a warriors courage and skill in battle.

After learning the Samurai's way of life and being nursed back to good health by the widow of the man he killed in battle, Nathan becomes a pseudo Samurai, and eventually helps lead them into battle against a better armed and more trained crop of "modern" Japanese soldiers.

From the moment you see Nathan, you can see where this is all going. Still, director Edward Zwick does a great job of showing the friendship that develops between Nathan and Katsumoto. And even though I think Nathan becomes a Samurai kind of fast, I thought the conflicts in the film were developed nicely.

Friendships and romance aside, I did expect to see more battles. I mean, *The Last Samurai* is a war film. But by the end of the film, I understood that the movie was more about Nathan's redemption for the bad that he did in the Civil War, as well as this period in Japanese history.

The Last Samurai is marked by a number of great performances. Cruise as Nathan Algren is believable. But I thought that Ken Watanabe gave the outstanding performance as Katsumoto, a noble Samurai at a changing time in Japanese history.

Because of its coverage of a piece of Japanese history that I was not aware of, and its performances and beautiful cinematography, *The Last Samurai* remains one of my favorite war films. But genre aside, *The Last Samurai* is a splendid film with great visuals and a good message. I give it three and a half-stars.

Gordon Parker, Jr.'s *Super Fly*: Superb Acting, Artistically Pleasing, and Aesthetically Satisfying, with Great Music

July 15, 2012 (age 16)

From the acting, to the musical score, to the writing, to the cinematography, *Super Fly* (1972), directed by Gordon Parks, Jr., is a film that will leave you in awe. Priest (Ron O'Neal) is a dope dealing king pin who's grown tired of all that's needed to retain his crown. He wants out! The drug game has gotten to him. He's having lady troubles. His "main man" is on the run. And his drug dealing partner is blinded by money. But before Priest gets out of the drug game for good, he needs to do one last score, a million dollar deal that'll secure the golden parachute he needs to start his new life with his lady Georgia (the incredibly beautiful Sheila Frazier). But when the police hears of his impressive drug dealing skills, Priest's way out turns into a dead end.

Ron O'Neal delivers a memorable performance as Priest. He's charismatic, smooth, and in control of every scene that he's in. Like the scene when two black nationalists try to shake him down for some money, he remains calm, all the while his finger's on the trigger of a gun beneath the table they're sitting at. But Priest isn't always smooth. No drug dealer has ever made it to the top by being soft. And Priest is no different. Take for instance the scene where Priest smacks down a gambler who interrupts a conversation between him and Eddie (Carl Lee).

Aside from Ron O'Neal, *Super Fly* features several other great (memorable) performances. Carl Lee is great as Eddie, Priest's partner. Although both gangsters are ruthlessly cool, Eddie's a sharp contrast to Priest. And nowhere is this more apparent than in the scene where Eddie is visibly more interested in making a partnership with a powerful group of corrupt police officers than Priest. Eddie's character is entrenched in the drug game and has no intentions of getting out, and Carl Lee plays this angle up perfectly, helping to create a natural conflict that's not resolved until the end of the film.

Julius Harris also delivers a solid performance as well. Harris plays "Scatter", a former kingpin and father figure to Priest. Looking for an opportunity to get out of the drug game himself, while helping Priest at the same time, Scatter teeters on the thin line between saving himself and getting out, or helping Priest escape as well. Scatter attempted to get out the game for good, but when Priest comes pleading he has to help. Unfortunately, however, by helping Priest, Scatter seals his own fate.

But acting isn't the only thing that makes *Super Fly* a masterpiece. The film is artistically pleasing and aesthetically satisfying as well. For example, *Super Fly* opens essentially with two long montages. The very first image we see are two junkies meeting up on a corner. One asks the other, "Did you get it?" The other replies in the negative, and the two take off walking. Set to Curtis Mayfield's song, "Little Child Runnin' Wild," the montage becomes a gritty walk through the early '70s Harlem ghetto. By song's end, the junkies' walk dissolves into a scene with Priest sitting up in the bed with one of his ladies.

Suddenly, Priest has to split; he has to go "make a pickup." He gets out of bed, gets dressed, and cut—he's in his car, driving uptown. Priest's drive up to Harlem begins the second extensive montage, which is set to instrumental version of Curtis Mayfield's song "Freddie's Dead." Priest arrives in Harlem, gets out of his car, and enters the apartment building previously entered by the junkies we saw earlier. Once inside, the junkies ambush Priest. There's a brief scuffle, the junkies rob Priest, and this leads to a grueling, on-foot chase scene.

Another artistic/aesthetic maneuver by director Gordon Parks, Jr. that impressed me was his use of still photography. Parks uses a montage of photography stills to effectively show elapsed time. Parks also uses the photography stills sequence to show the progress and success of Priest's operation. The stills were a creative and rather effective way of moving the story along without using any dialogue or live action.

Now, I would be remiss if I didn't talk about *Super Fly's* musical score. A classic score composed by one of the most revered and respected soul artists of all time, Curtis Mayfield. Sometimes used as a virtual narrator, music plays a huge role in the grand scheme of things in *Super Fly*. Mayfield repeatedly pours soulful peroxide inside the cut that is Super Fly. Whether it be moving the story along or serving as a quasi narrator, music is essentially the soul of the film.

Super Fly is one of the greatest films I've ever seen. Although it's often referred to as a "blaxploitation" film (a term that does this film no justice), I see *Super Fly* just as I do any other well-made gangster film. *Super Fly* is a well rounded, well executed, cinematic force. It's artistically sound, with excellent acting, top-notch cinematography, and the music is fantastically beautiful. *Super Fly* will always be a monumental film in my life and film studies. I give it four stars.

Other Wrtitings

Sam Greenlee's *Ammunition*, Superb Writing

January 2, 2010 (age 13)

This weekend, I got my first book of poetry, *Ammunition* by author Sam Greenlee. To say the least, this book of poetry is great! Sam Greenlee's writing style is crazy and rhythmic. Reading *Ammunition* has already helped me improve my own writing and speech rhythm. For this to be my first poetry book, I don't think I could've had a better pick. Thank you, Pop! I really like this book and all of the poems in it. I probably have a post-it note on every page, marking all the poems that I like.

Even though I finished reading *Ammunition* in a day, believe me I took my time. Whether it be a short or long poem, Greenlee's writing was consistent. His poems touch on a lot of topics that I would like to delve further into. I think Greenlee's word choice is on a next level. *Ammunition* is simply a great book. I recommend reading this book of poetry to anybody, even if you're not into writing all that much. I look forward to reading more of Greenlee's writings.

Live Sports Can Advance the Human Mind

November 5, 2010 (age 14)

Live sports can go either way. One team is ultimately going to win. But while watching, you can learn a lot. You also get to witness how certain minds work when put into pressure situations. Live sports isn't just entertainment, and shouldn't be treated as such. Instead, there should be constant analyzing, studying, and talk about the sport while it's going on. My favorite sport, is American football. However, baseball is a close second.

When watching Football, play-calling is an important thing to pay attention to. Players roles are detailed, and must be executed perfectly in order for each call to work effectively. If anything goes wrong, it could mean devastation. With all of these variables involved, they make for a good thinking game. Sort of like Chess, attack, and counter-attack. A lot of thought is put into each play. In the end, whoever wins, called the best plays at the most opportune times. And the loser, however, often has to improve their play-calling,

Baseball is completely different. Plays are called, sure. But not to the meticulous degree that they're called in football. Baseball is a pitch by pitch game that moves slow, with some small fast moments here and there. With baseball, the batter and the pitcher are both working against each other. The pitcher is trying to get the batter out by calling the right pitch, while the batter is trying to guess which pitch is coming. Whenever the pitcher or batter anticipates correctly, they have a better chance of being successful. The pitcher has a lot more thinking to do than a batter. The pitcher has to think of a pitch to call in each situation, then he has to think of what the batter expects is coming,

Managers, not quite the equivalent to head coaches in football, play an important role, too. The manager has to decide in the beginning and during the game what position players he wants on the field. And when it comes to managing, all managers have their own styles to playing the game. I think baseball and football both have their similarities. I'm just more inclined to football because of how much more control and responsibility the players are given in each situation.

Sports may be considered just entertainment, but to me, it's much more. I value watching sports (especially with my father) and analyzing the many things I would do. It helps my "Situational Awareness." Plus, if you're watching your favorite team, it can also be fun. You want that team to win, and you think about the best options available for them to succeed. More importantly, live sports come in handy for quick brain exercises, as well as entertainment.

Editor's note: As of 2012, Amir's favorite sport is now world Football (soccer)

"Course of Empire," Favorite Painting from Thomas Cole

November 11, 2011 (age 15)

Before I went to the New York Historical Society for the first time, I had never heard of the Painter Thomas Cole. But in the first week at one of my classes there, I got to see one of Cole's most famous paintings, The Course Of Empire. The Course Of Empire is a five-part series of paintings created by Cole over a span of three years (1833-1836). This series of paintings show different stages of human civilization. The paintings also give a glimpse into what Americans believed Empires would ultimately lead to.

The series of paintings depicts the rise and fall of an imaginary city. A city that is marked by a huge boulder overlooking the valley in every painting. The Course of Empire paintings have lots of intricate details that can be discussed for hours. Like the boulder that shows up in each painting, the color scheme, etc., literally each painting could have it's own class.

When you take a look at The Course Of Empire it's fun to try to figure out and discuss the order of the paintings. The order is kind of tricky. Each painting could actually be first or last, but certain details give you clues to the right order. The first time that I took a look at the paintings, I got the order correct. But before I gave an answer, I considered at least three different orders.

From all of the paintings I've seen (about 30 so far over the past few weeks), I'd have to say The Course Of Empire is my favorite. I categorize it as one painting because of the name, even though it's really a series. It's my favorite painting because of the intricate details and story behind the painting. Also, I like the color contrast in the first and fourth pictures within the series.

The first painting depicts civilization in it's earliest state. There's a lot of trees and grass. There are also limited humans, and those shown are portrayed as "savages" or hunter gatherers. I also liked seeing the Native Americans and Tipis, and how the sea was a part of the landscape and seemed to be the backdrop along with the boulder.

In the fourth painting, there's a lot of things going on. In each part of the painting you can see something different. For example, colors are bright and dim in certain spots. There are also a lot of detailed people and objects flying that can be hard to manage. Plus, they can also be hard to paint. Nonetheless, Cole did a good job of capturing the essence of a falling empire.

Since seeing The Course Of Empire painting, I've only seen two other Cole paintings. Both caught my attention, but didn't capture the same reaction. But the paintings collectively did inspire me to write an article about Cole's work.

It, First Stephen King Novel More Creepier than Any Film Adaptation of His Work

February 11, 2011 (age 14)

After reading *It*, my first Stephen King book, a lot of my pre-conceived notions were assured. I've arrived at the conclusion that, *It*, by itself, is scarier than any two film adaptations of King's Books! I saw *Christine* and *The Shining*. Those are two scary films. But to me, they were outdone by only two or three chapters of reading *It*.

It is written in a style that is much scarier than any film adaptation could ever really be. And the things that you imagine from King's descriptions are much worse than any that could be presented on the big screen.

It is the story of a clown. A clown who terrorizes kids of all ages. And he does his job very well. His techniques originate from using simple blue or orange balloons to engage his prey. This clown isn't ordinary, either. He disguises himself in order to hunt and pounce on his victims. He appears in small-towns. And where would a mysterious, creepy clown like this reside? The sewer of course! The place where nobody would look, the place where the deaths would be quiet. And what's this clown's name? It's Bob Gray, or should I say, Pennywise The Dancing Clown...

From the moment you enter the story misdirection takes a strong hold of you. Not knowing what you're getting into with *It*, the early horror will have your mind shifting. Listen to me: Reading a book of its stature requires preparation. You must be prepared to read some of the most scary, crazy horror shit you have ever read. When I began reading *It*, I will admit, I wasn't prepared. The only thing I knew of the book was that Stephen King wrote it. Little did I know how detailed the events would be.

First Mixing Session Goes Well: Microphone Adjustment Turned Music Lesson

December 23, 2010 (age 14)

I always liked making beats with my father (Amir Said AKA Sa'id). I learn a lot, and it's fun. Plus, I get to help Pop create his beats. He teaches me how to sample, which I find really helpful. I like samples just as much as he does. Sometimes, when Pop is making a beat, he'll let me play the beat and/or rhyme over it. He also might let me add something to his beat, or allow me to make my own beat, and I get to practice using our MPC 4000. But above all, as of today, I've got a new found job—assistant mix engineer to Pop.

Today, Pop and I began a session where we mixed his vocals from a song he made. For the majority of the time, Pop was instructing me on how to do it. Initially, the lesson was given in order for me to put into action sometime in the future. But after we realized we'd rather just continue our session, we kept on going. To the point where Pop and I did three or four runs of vocals. Each time around, we altered something different in order to find out where we needed to be. Eventually, I learned a lot about the basics of mixing and mixed my first set of vocals!

Mixing, rhyming, and creating beats are three separate things. Each component has its own level of toughness. But when it comes to mixing, I think a few minor mistakes can be made that'll undo the whole project, especially when it comes to vocals. I learned early on that there are different volume settings, techniques, and audio settings that play a part in effective vocals. I also learned that when doing vocals, it matters how close or far apart you are from the microphone. Another thing, probably the most important, it's not easy to learn the basics of mixing vocals. If you plan on attempting to do it, make sure you have an instructor who teaches well.

Making beats with Pop isn't just about learning how; the same goes with rhyming. It's a special thing for me. I take it seriously, and I'm enthusiastic about it whenever I have the chance. Making beats and rhyming over them is something that Pop is very good at, just like writing. So with both crafts, I try to get as much information as I can to get better. This is a great experience every time, and I hope to continue this until I grow up.

Literary Club Very Special to Me

January 24, 2010 (age 13)

As a kid, I felt like I belonged wherever I went. For example, I felt like I belonged at my grandmother's house. But the fact of the matter is, I didn't know any better. You can't always belong everywhere you go. There are some places you go that you simply won't feel comfortable at, or you won't like the atmosphere. I bring this up to make a point. Last Friday, when I went to my new literary club, was the third time that I felt like I really belonged somewhere. (Laurie Spigel runs the literary club for homeschoolers. Thanks Laurie.)

This was the first time that I ever joined a literary club. I thought everyone in literary club was really cool. A group of people coming together to discuss books and their thoughts, that's dope! I was the newest member of the literary club, and I was welcomed immediately by everyone. I felt like I really belonged there. It seemed like everyone was an instant friend.

Needless to say, literary club is cool. My first time there, we discussed *A Tale of Two Cities*. We discussed different themes in great detail, and we went practically chapter by chapter. I won't say exactly what we talked about because that would include spoilers. Bottom line: I found literary club to be really beneficial, not only because I learned things about the book and the story that I never even thought about, but because I know it will help me with my own writing. Literary club is great.

The Oscars Offer an Opportunity to Learn

March 8, 2010 (age 13)

I watch the Oscars to learn. When watching, I learn about three things mainly. First, I gain insight into the film business. When watching, I pay attention to all the award winners, especially when they give their speeches. If you listen carefully, they often give a lot of insight into the film business, and the names of people that you should know. And there are other little things that award winners say that can give you insight into the business. Whether it be A-list or C-List actors, writers, and directors, they can all drop jewels in their speeches. For example, just watching last night, an award winner, I can't remember who, said that they'd been "stuck in development all their life." This means that all their projects where "in development," and never actually completed or green lighted. That's revealing; tells you something about how hard it is to get projects made in the movie industry.

The second thing I learn is some people's character. When watching, I learn a lot from people's facial expressions. Let's say an actor, actress, director, or writer wins and a fellow actor actress, etc. doesn't stand up to clap. That shows me how that person feels and how they react to other people winning besides them. That shows conceit and jealously, traits that I'm not fond of.

The third thing I learn is how the Academy feels about every movie. I learn this through the selections made by the Academy for each film category. Sometimes I agree with the Academy's choices, and sometimes I disagree with them. However, it's what they decide, and I gain insight into how certain types of movies are usually received. These are just some reasons why the Oscars are cool.

Maus, Intriguing Holocaust True Story Told through the Eyes of Mice

May 10, 2010 (age 14)

I've started to read the graphic novel *Maus* by Art Spiegelman. This book is crazy. The story is based on the struggle of Spiegelman's father (Vladek Spiegelman) to survive the Holocaust as a Polish Jew. Most of the story is told through his father's memory. But here's the catch. All the people in the book are represented by animals. The Jews are represented by mice, the Nazi's are represented by Cats and the Americans are represented by dogs. I think this use of animals to portray this story is very creative.

Vladek's story is very interesting. I've never read a story about a Holocaust survivor before, but this story is engaging and informative. Through all of his vivid memories you as a reader feel sad for each character. Plus, Vladek breaks down everything that happened, including the how and when. I've read about 130 pages of book one and it's hard to stop. I highly recommend this book. One more thing, this book will most likely get you hooked on graphic novels.

HTML and CSS Coding Intense Work

May 5, 2010 (age 14)

Learning CSS and HTML code is fun. Just in case you didn't notice, I revamped my blog and made it three columns, along with a few minor changes. It's part of a design that I wanted to change to. But the best part was learning how. I'll start off by saying, its A LOT of code. There are so many different things that you have to do. The thing is, if you're one space off with code it can ruin your whole site. All the code has to be precise and correct. Then there's the separate templates.

All of the different templates have code that need to be started from scratch if you really want to customize your blog. These templates are part of the "Advanced" template that Typepad offers. This Advanced Template is only for those users who know code, and know how to use it. When learning how to use HTML code its not easy at all, it takes a lot of time. I have a new understanding of why programmers and website creators are paid so much by the hour because of the intense work that they put in.

Baseball and Enchiladas

January 30, 2010 (age 13)

Yesterday was jam-packed. But it was a great day! Pop and I went to get batting gear for the batting cages, and afterwards, we got enchilada ingredients. Here's a breakdown of how the day went.

At around 2pm, Pop and I went to Modell's Sporting Goods. At Modell's, we searched for a bat. Finally, we settled on a Nike one. It was a black and red Keystone model. My bat was 32 inches by 21 ounces. After picking out my bat, we looked for a helmet. We got a Nike helmet. Then it was time to get cleats. You might ask what company this time? Nike of course. Lastly, it was time to get batting gloves, and we went with Nike again. Once we left Modell's, we went home and started watching a movie on TCM (Turner Classic Movies). We watched *The Baron Of Arizona.* That movie truly deserves a film review from me.

After the movie, we went to the batting cages at the 3rd Avenue Sportscenter. When we got there, Pop bought a handful of video game tokens by mistake. Once we realized, we got the correct tokens and went to the batting cages. I started off (and ended) at just 45 mph. It was just for warm-up anyway, but man was it a work out. I hadn't hit a baseball for a year, since I'd gave up baseball for good. Man, it felt good. It was a great experience, getting my stroke back. But it took about two rounds of batting practice to hit one ball. My mechanics and stance were way off, but eventually I got it together. By the end, I felt good about my batting practice.

After batting practice, Pop and I went on a journey to find enchilada ingredients for dinner. We went to a couple of supermarkets in Park Slope, even a corner store in Sunset

Park. Eventually, we just stopped off at Pathmark. Funny! They had everything we needed for a delicious meal. Once we got home, Pop made the enchiladas. Those enchiladas that Pop made may very well be the best dinner he's ever made! It was so good. It was such a full day, and to have a meal like that just capped off a wonderful day. This is the kind of stuff I look forward to doing.

"I Seen It All," My Favorite Song by Screwball

June 8, 2010 (age 14)

Screwball's "I Seen It All" is one of the best songs I've ever heard. I like "I Seen It All" mainly for two reasons, the beat and the lyrics. The beat is laid back, it's a real subtle, murky type of beat. The song starts off with a murky horn with a sample of Guru (of Gang Starr) speaking, then another sample of someone else speaking. Then DJ Premier (of Gang Starr) drops a strong, yet simple kick and snare pattern. For the rest of the song the beat rides out like that. And when it comes time for the hook, the beat is lowered and the vocals are raised.

Then the lyrics come in. The lyrics are simple like the beat may appear to be, but like the beat, the lyrics hit, too. Everybody who rhymes tells their own story. The raspy nature and aggressiveness in the rappers' voice makes this song go hard. All of them ride the beat and make the song even better. All of the stories told in the song come back to the title, "I Seen It All." In effect, they're all describing what they've seen, and the hook reveals it the most.

***The River*, Engaging Survival Tale: Sequel To *Hatchet* Almost Better Than the Original**

February 13, 2011 (age 14)

About a year or two ago, I read *Hatchet* by Gary Paulsen. It was a very engaging survival tale surrounding a boy named Brian Robeson. Brian is stranded in the Canadian wilderness after the pilot of the plane he was traveling in has a heart-attack. Brian's forced to land the plane by himself, too bad he crashed into a lake near-by and just barely made it out alive.

Hatchet is one of those, "keep-you-on-the-edge-of-your-seat" type of books. Needless to say, when I first read it, I didn't know that this was the first book in a series. I thought *Hatchet* was the only book Gary Paulsen wrote.

Yesterday, I finished reading *The River*, part two in the *Hatchet* series. The twist that was introduced in the beginning had me shocked. I had no clue what direction the story was going to go in. But I certainly didn't expect what I read within the first 10 pages. From reading *The River*, I can't wait to read the remaining two sequels. If they prove to be any thing similar to *The River*, then the *Hatchet* series may be one of the best I've read.

I've read about ten Gary Paulsen books, and I plan on reading more. The *Hatchet* series just goes to show his range. However, I think most of his stories have something to do with him and where he grew up. He's written survival stories before, and he's practically carved his own spot in that style of writing. Besides *A Series of Unfortunate Events* (my favorite book series), the *Hatchet* series would have to be a close second.

Literary Club: *Anna Karenina* Book Discussions and Great Surprises

April 30, 2010 (age 14)

In literary club this past Friday, we discussed parts four through six in *Anna Karenina* by Leo Tolstoy. We went over major themes, storylines, and each main character. In *Anna Karenina*, death and love are huge themes that surround practically every chapter. In fact, part six is titled "Death" (it also happens to be the only part titled in the book). In the story there are two couples and an affair with parallel relationships. However, throughout the story you see the relationships go in three different directions. The affair only gets depressing by the page number, but Anna can't turn back to her husband because that relationship is even worse. So what is she left to do?

Through the discussion, I realized that ultimately somebody's going to die. We went over all of the characters, and came to the conclusion that one person is going to commit suicide. I agreed because there are too many variables to lead me to believe that this particular character won't. If you ever read *Anna Karenina*, you'll know exactly who I'm talking about within the first three parts.

Anna Karenina is a very engaging story. Tolstoy takes his time laying out the story. As the book progresses, it only gets better. Each character is given incredible care and detail, to the point where one character is modeled after Tolstoy. This story is way beyond what I expected it to be, I think this book will blow most people away. I only hope that you can handle it, and you continue to read until the end. Believe me, it's worth it.

Side Note: I went to literary club with one book, *Anna Karenina*, and I came back home with nine more books!

That's just one great thing about literary club. There are always cool surprises, like Laurie giving me books that she thinks I'll dig. Besides that, the discussions are always great and I learn a lot. That's why whenever you read a book, you should always discuss what you've read.

TV Land and TCM: Classic Television Shows and Films Important to the Television and Film Industry

November 24, 2010 (age 14)

Lately, I've taken a lot of interest in watching the cable channel TV Land. TV Land offers a lot of old (classic) T.V. shows from a variety of different eras. For example, "Bonanza" (1950s), "All in the Family" (1970s), and "Sanford and Son" (1970s). Each show has their own angle at life, which corresponds to their respective periods. Each show also holds their own weight in my film and television vault. But the most important thing is that a channel like TV Land exists on cable.

TV Land is preserving classic T.V. shows. Each show that's preserved is forever in rotation for new generations. Also, the shows on TV land serve as reference material for writers, directors, and other artists. Other T.V. Shows, plays, films, and books could be created using things found in these older shows that TV Land airs. But TV Land is not the only cable channel dealing in the preservation market. Turner Classic Movies (TCM) is another great channel that airs older works. However, TCM specializes in classic films. I think both TV Land and TCM do a great job of preserving great works for future audiences.

Eventually, I think there will be an influx of filmmakers, T.V. producers, and writers who reach far back for inspiration. As stories become even more cliché and dialogue more boring and uninteresting, I think the above mentioned groups will be desperate for new material. By that time, they'll be scrambling for ideas. Now, what's a better place to start than the 50s, 60s, and 70s? To me, that's the meat of most well written shows and films.

More Girls, Ain't No Problem for Me

February 1, 2009 (age 12)

Yesterday, I went to my friend Katelyn's 13th birthday party. It was mad fun. I danced with a lot of girls. I got to the party early again, and I got to stay much longer. But I think Pop was doing something, he didn't come to pick me up until about 11:15 P.M. But hey, it didn't make no never mind to me. Most of the people that were at the party were girls, which is actually better, because you get more dances. Katelyn had a lot of contemporary music, Spanish music towards the end, and Biggie qualified as her "back in the day" music. I didn't dance to any Spanish music because I got tired by the end of the party. But when some of the reggae and today's music came on, I wasn't tired anymore.

I danced with Suzzane, Liza and Kaira (the twins), Chandra, Imani, Destiny, Kharene, Rochelle, Tiana, and many others. We finally got to the cake at a little after 10. And again, just like the last party I went to, the birthday girl got smacked in the face with cake!

Now, this time I got to stay for the semi-slow jams and the real slow jams. And my theory was proven: slow jams bring out the grown up inside of girls... When I got home, I was mad tired. This time not because of soda, but I was still out of it.

Lakers Tap Mike Brown; Questionable Coaching Choice

May 27, 2011 (age 15)

The Lakers have found their new coach. Former Cleveland Cavaliers head coach, Mike Brown, signed a four year deal two days ago. You may remember the name Mike Brown because he presided over some of Lebron's best years as an NBA player. Back then, Lebron James was a piece of raw, untapped, great Akron, Ohio talent. Lebron lead the Cavs to multiple playoff appearances. But I don't think Brown had that much to do with The Cavs' success.

Whenever I watched the Cavs play, Mike Brown appeared to just sit on the sideline and watch. Didn't seem like there was any coaching going on at all. Mike Brown and the Cavs front office rode Lebron's success and talent, not Mike Brown's coaching, to their team's success. But there didn't appear to be any coaching or front office support around Lebron. Case in point, Mike Brown didn't do anything to help his superstar get some help on the team. In fact, last year, Lebron decided to "take his talents to South Beach," and sign with the Miami Heat. Mike Brown was fired during the 2010 off-season. And Now, he's the coach of the Los Angeles Lakers? What the fuck were the Lakers smoking?

I don't think the Lakers front office used their brains on this one. AT ALL! Looks like they didn't pick Kobe Bryant's brain either. Instead, they went ahead and just hired Mike Brown without talking to Kobe first.

The Kobe Bryant era is coming to a close. Kobe will be 33 when the 2012 season starts. That leaves the Lakers with just about three or four years to find the next All-Star to lead the team. But with the last few years, that they can still get out of Kobe, there are still pieces missing around him. Down the road, he needs to groom someone to takeover.

I don't see that person on the Lakers roster.

The Lakers are on the cusp of re-building. The Mike Brown era is beginning. Phil Jackson is leaving. Pau Gasol proved in the playoffs how soft he really is; and he will be 31 when next season starts. Lamar Odom and Ron Artest will turn 32 during next season. And Derek Fisher will be 37. The Lakers have a old squad. Whether it's though free agency or the upcoming NBA Draft, the Lakers need to get younger. And Mike Brown presiding over this re-building team will not work! Remember, The Cavs didn't trust him enough to rebuild theirs.

Editor's note: The Lakers fired Mike Brown just after a 1-4 start.

Finished Reading *David Copperfield*; Payed Off Big Time: Another Charles Dickens Novel Demonstrates His Eloquent and Detailed

November 7, 2010 (age 14)

I had *David Copperfield* sitting on one of my book shelves for at least six months now. On a casual trip to go get some gummy bears on one of my writing breaks, I came across *David Copperfield.* I also noticed another Charles Dickens novel, *Great Expectations.* At that moment I had a decision to make. Which book would be next in my reading queue? After about three to five minutes of thought, I concluded that I'd start off with *David Copperfield.*

The story of *David Copperfield* deals with the life of a child named David Copperfield. The story follows Copperfield from his childhood to adulthood. Copperfield had a happy childhood, living with his mother and nurse Peggotty. David doesn't live with his father because he died six months before his birth. But when his mother re-marries Edward Murdstone, Copperfield doesn't like his new stepfather. Edward beats David for falling behind in school. When Copperfield bites his stepfather during one of these beatings, he's sent to boarding school.

Ever since I first read *A Tale of Two Cities*, I became a Charles Dickens fan. Dickens is unlike any writer I've ever read. I like the way Dickens writes and utilizes details to get his stories across. Dickens doesn't waste words, but he sure knows how to elaborate upon one topic endlessly. His style of writing is so precise, and he never fails to keep his readers engaged. Of all the writers I've read, Dickens is certainly one of my favorites.

David Copperfield's storyline is simple but with layers upon layer of support. The way Copperfield's character was portrayed had a great deal to do with Dickens himself. Somehow in each one of his stories, Dickens has at least one character who has his attributes. This book was practically an autobiography. Dickens life was similar to that of David Copperfield, and that was intentional. Nonetheless, I liked *David Copperfield.*

I dig fiction and especially mysteries. I also like stories that take time to develop. *David Copperfield* is a perfect example since it spans over three quarters of one person's life. I liked how the storyline was executed and I wonder how the story would've turned out if it continued past the ending. *David Copperfield* is a classic, one of Dickens' best works. I look forward to reading more of his books.

A Day in Film School

February 14, 2009 (age 12)

Today in my film workshop at the New York Film Academy (NYFA), we learned about the art of directing. Specifically, when Bart, our instructor, added to my knowledge of a film shot. He gave a definition that I never thought of before. Shots are a visual choice that the director makes by motivation and a clear Point of View that focuses on telling the story of the movie. Shots should not be about how beautiful or impressive, but should be about the story. We also learned about shot types and the 180 degree rule. The 180 degree rule is when a shot can go no further than 180 degrees. One interesting shot is "Mise en scene". That means one scene with no edits for one shot.

We also learned about camera angles. Camera angles are the position of the camera to the vertical subject. A vertical subject is a person or place. The most common camera angles are: Eye level, High Angle, and Low Angle. Eye level is neutral to the level of the subject or normal. High Angle is above the eye level. Directors use High Angles to make the subject look smaller and more diminutive (just learned this word today!). Low angle is below the eye level. This angle makes the subject look bigger, stronger, and signifies power.

We also learned about composition as well. Composition is to compose the shot of the subject on a horizontal plane. Composition is another way of saying location. There are three types of location: foreground, midground, and background. Foreground is below, and midground is in the middle, and background is in the back. There are three composition types: frontal, angled view, and basic shot types. Frontal is often used for comedy, it's not dramatic and it gives a 2D look. Angled view gives a 3D look, it's often used for more drama, tension, realism, and more visual information. Basic shot types are single (one subject), double (two subjects), group shots, and over the shoulder shots. I'll most likely be using angled view and over the shoulder shots, since that's what I like the most. But I'll still have to learn about all of them because I want to be able to do all of them well.

Then we learned about camera movement. We learned about dolly, which is smooth movement and the camera moves on a track. "Stedicam" is attached to an arm and the operator can walk with the camera while the arm absorbs the shocks of walking. "Handheld" is when the camera is held by the operator. "Pan" is moving the camera left to right and tracking shot is when a camera tracks on a dolly in a car.

The last thing we learned about was lenses. Their are three types of lenses: wide lens, normal (medium) lens, and telephoto lens. Wide lens captures the width of the shot. It also captures a lot of info, it has a great depth of field and small numbers. A telephoto lens has large numbers, it brings the subject closer, and it creates intimacy with the audience.

Today was a great day at film school. I took in a lot of information. Our instructor, Bart Mastronardi, is a good teacher. He was able to give good notes, allow us to work hands on, and help everyone understand what we learned. Most of the information, I learned I had no clue about, even though I've acted on a real film set before. But now I have a lot of knowledge, which I'll need for the future.

The Rise and Fall of Greg Paulus

March 26, 2009 (age 13)

"Oh, boy, this kid Paulus is a star, baby, did you see that crossover?" says Dick Viatle. "You know Dick, most people dribble with two hands, but this kid knows how to dribble with one," says the announcer who joins in with the ass-kissing and over hype of Greg Paulus.

I might be exaggerating (just a little) to get my point across. Duke guard, Greg Paulus, was a star last year. Now he's just a bench player, and not one that dominates. If Greg Paulus came out last year and entered the draft, he would've been a 1st round pick off all of the hype. But this year, he's just a bench player that plays at Duke, and everyone gets to see how good he really is. Oh, that's right, he's *not* that good! This year, Duke Basketball revolves around Kyle Singler, John Scheyer, and Gerald Henderson. Paulus gets no attention and nobody hypes him up anymore.

This year, you might hear something like, "Paulus passes the ball. You know, this kid Paulus used to be really good, but this year he's whack!" Once again, I exaggerate (a little). But Greg Paulus is not going to be drafted if you ask me. I don't think he'll be picked up as a free agent. What does he add to an NBA team? A bench warmer? So look for Paulus to go the route of former star guard Omar Cook. Remember him?

Editor's note: Greg Paulus entered the 2009 NBA draft. He was not drafted. In 2011, he was hired as the video coordinator for the Ohio State University mens basketball team.

Deniece Williams' "Silly" Could Teach My Generation Something About Music

April 26, 2010 (age 14)

Today was the first day that I heard "Silly" by Deniece Williams. I heard it before when I was much younger. But this was the first time I listened to it and studied it on my own. It's such a beautiful song. The way that Deniece Williams sings engages the listener. Even how the song starts off, the vocals don't come in until around the :30 second mark. It's a slow moving, cool melody to introduce the song. After 30 seconds in, Deniece Williams comes in with the vocals in a low pitch tone. She sings the opening verse and then goes into the change during the hook.

"Silly" is a nice, mood-swinging song. Meaning, however you were just feeling, the song just takes you on a journey and puts you in a better mood. The way her voice moves in and out of the music engages you. She easily changes the pitch of her voice, both subtly and aggressively, whenever she needs to.

Even though I'm 14 years old, music like this will always stick with me. Other kids in my generation will listen to Beyonce or Rihanna, but I find refuge in listening to Aretha Franklin and Gladys Knight. I think that if kids in my generation were to listen to the music I listen to, they would like it. I also think that would change the way other kids in my generation think, thereby creating an offspring of children who preserve this kind of music. But instead, music like this isn't played in rotation over the radio or on the iPods of kids in my generation.

Lazy Dog, Dum Dums, and War Metals! Oh, My!

December 22, 2009 (age 13)

Going into Social Studies class today, I knew we were going to see some weapons from World War I (WWI). I was looking forward to seeing all of the different weapons that my teacher brought in from WWI. Then, there was an announcement, "All 8th Grade Homerooms, kindly report to the Auditorium, thank you." That SABOTAGED everything! Once my class got downstairs, we waited for about 10 minutes, just to be notified by another announcement that, "The Assembly has been canceled and rescheduled, sorry for the inconvenience. May all 8th Grade Homerooms please report back to class." If I decided to describe my anger, it wouldn't be such a great idea, so I'll continue.

Once my class finally returned, we immediately started the lesson, since we already lost a lot of time. We started off learning about the words squadron and "Ace". Then, we went into the airplane used by America during WWI and the weapons used. A squadron is a group of six to seven airplanes. An "Ace" is a pilot that is able to shoot down 5 or more enemy planes. The "Ace" was seen differently throughout the world. Each major nation in the war had its own standards for their fighter pilots. Germany didn't allow their fighter pilots to gain the "Ace" title until they shot down 20 enemy planes! France and Great Britain also had their own standards. America probably had the lowest standards for their fighter pilots' high ranking.

The Speed and Altitude level of the airplane dramatically changed over a four year period. In 1914, the airplane could only fly up to 80 MPH, could reach 12,000 feet in altitude and could only fly for two hours. By 1918, the airplane could fly up to 125 MPH, could reach 19,000 feet in altitude, and fly for four hours. Also, airplanes had the M2 Machine Gun, Browning .50 Caliber Machine Gun attached to the top of the plane. It shot 450-600 rpm (Rounds Per Minute). However, the gun jammed easily, so if it happened to jam on you, the fight was over, and you where going down. The airplane was really bulky and big, but over the years it improved.

It's time to announce the six out of about ten weapons my class should've seen (see paragraph 1). My class saw three medals handed out to fighter pilots. The Medals where given from America, Germany, and France. These medals were incredibly cool. We also saw the "hat" that American fighter pilots wore. Then we saw a round of Machine Gun casings, along with four bullets left from the Browning .50 Caliber Machine Gun. I think that was the best thing we saw, those bullet casings and bullets looked incredible. I've never seen bullets like that before, but if you got hit with one of those, it sure would do some damage. The last thing we saw was the Lazy Dog. The Lazy Dog was a small bomb during WWI. This little bomb did a lot of damage. As you may know, usually in a fighter plane, two people are there. One in the front flying, and the other in the back watching the tail and shooting. Well the person in the back also had another job: to empty boxes upon boxes of Lazy Dogs onto the battlefield. This little bomb falling from 12,000 feet would instantly kill a wandering soldier. All of these weapons/medals were great, but I think the Machine Gun casings and bullets, and the American medal were the best.

My social studies teacher said he bought most of those items at Army auctions, and I sure feel like taking a trip to one of them. These items are cool and valuable and they tell a lot of history. Tomorrow I look forward to seeing more weapons, if there isn't another assembly or assembly malfunction.

The Yankees Let One Slip Away, Lose Game to Angels they Should Have Won

December 22, 2009 (age 13)

The Yankees had a 4 run lead through three innings, then the fifth inning came. The Yankees were cruising throughout this game. Through three, Angel pitcher, Saunders was struggling and just serving up pitches to the Yankee batters. But he was able to make it through 5 innings with a 5-1 deficit. However, nobody knew what was going to happen in the next two innings.

In the bottom of the fifth inning, the Yankees were beating the Angels 5-1. Then Chone Figgins singled, and stole second. But from a witness standpoint (Pop), Figgins was out, even though the second base umpire called him safe. That would've been one out. Then, Izturis fouled out to Jose Molina, bringing up Bobby Abreu. During this at-bat, Abreu brought in Chone Figgins with a single, and like Figgins, Abreu stole second. Then, Juan Rivera came up and was able to reach because of an A-Rod error. The next batter was Kendry Morales. On a full-count, Morales hit a three-run home-run to tie the game at 5. The Angels weren't done.

In the sixth inning, Erick Aybar led off with a single. Followed by a Chone Figgins triple that brought in Aybar. After Figgins's triple, Izturis grounded out to Yankees pitcher, Melancon. However, Bobby Abreu came up and brought in another run with a single. Then Juan Rivera came up and grounded into a double-play. This left the score at 7-5.

In the 7th inning, the Yankees tried to strike back. Teixeira led off with a single, followed by a A-Rod strikeout. Then, Nick Swisher flied out, followed by a Robinson Cano single. Next, Melky Cabera hit a single, bringing in Teixeira to make the score 7-6. Then, the Yankees sent up Jorge Posada, who was walked to make the bases loaded. Next up was Hideki Matsui, who popped out. He sent the right fielder to the warning track, I thought it was a grand slam.

In the bottom of the 7th, the Angels finished off the Yankees. Kendry Morales led off with a ground out. Then the catcher, Napoli, came up and was safe off of a Jeter error. Next, Matthews Jr. grounded out, moving Napoli to second. Then Mathis was walked after Brian Bruney was brought in the game. The next batter was Erick Aybar, and he gave the final blow, a three-run home-run, giving the Angels a 10-6 lead. After the 7th inning, all scoring came to an end, giving the Anaheim Angels the win.

Mark Twain's *Adventures of Huckleberry Finn* In Reading Queue; Classic American Literature Loaded with History

January 13, 2011 (age 14)

The first Mark Twain book I'm reading is *Adventures of Huckleberry Finn*. One of the most important books in American Literature sits on my bookshelf, and I'm just now reading it. After yesterday, I'd read the introduction, written by John Seelye, and thirty pages. To say the least, *Adventures of Huckleberry Finn* isn't anything near what I thought. It took me about ten pages to get adapted to the writing style, setting, and feel of the book. I realized that certain grammar and word choices were made according to the time and characters. Once I got past that part, I was able to dive into the book.

Since I started reading *Adventures of Huckleberry Finn*, I don't think there's a page that doesn't have yellow ink. I'm highlighting practically every other sentence or paragraph! The main reason why I'm highlighting so much is because I plan on reading this book a number of times. I plan on understanding as much as I can from this classic so that I can participate in multiple discussions, as well as for my own use. I don't think I'm the only person who wonders why this book was written in this fashion. I'm also not the only one who wants to know the history of this book and its relationship with the time it was published.

The book's release in the late 1800s, after the Civil War is interesting. Twain has a backstory of his own regarding the Civil War and his life. I don't plan on going into that now. However, I think it's important to note that Twain said that his views on major topics regarding the Civil War changed and developed over his lifetime. I think that may be why this book was written on a rather radical slant. Still, I believe that Twain's style of writing is just as great as Dickens. Both writers use heavy prose, intricate details, and realistic characters. A comparison between the two would be interesting.

Adventures of Huckleberry Finn is one of those rare, timeless writing masterpieces. It's a book that is widely adored in literature and is studied by many. I'm a new reader thrown into the mix. This book is going to kick off a heavy rotation of Mark Twain literature that I hope to gain a lot from. So far, I've already begun eating up this book as if it's an information hub. Twain is a classic writer that I think warrants every writer's attention. Plus, *Adventures of Huckleberry Finn* is like a history lesson, great fiction, and prose all in one.

Arties, *Ponyo*, and Borders Equals a Great Sunday

April 10, 2009 (age 13)

Yesterday, I went to Symphony Space with my mother to see *Ponyo*, a movie by Hayao Miyazaki, a Japanese filmmaker. We also went to Arties, a famous deli located on Broadway and 83rd St. The last place we went to was Borders located near Columbus Circle. At Borders, I got five new books: *The Audacity of Hope* by Barack Obama, *Nickle and Dimed* by Barbara Ehrenreich, *The Hardy Boys book 11 and 12* by Franklin W. Dixon, and *The River* by Gary Paulsen.

Before my mother and I went to see *Ponyo*, we attended Arties for lunch. At Arties I had a Roast Beef sandwich and chicken fingers along with french fries. Man, those fries and chicken fingers were banging! The Roast Beef sandwich looked so good and was so big that I had to take it home to eat it. My mother had a Brisket of Beef sandwich and she ate about half of that. Arties' food certainly hit the spot. And I liked Arties's overall atmosphere, it was a good experience, and I plan on going again. After lunch, we headed over to Symphony Space.

Before the movie began, there was a long line outside, about 50 minutes before the movie was suppose to start. Once we came inside, we immediately took in the auditorium, it was huge! Then we quickly grabbed seats since so many people where there. It was so packed that before the movie began, half of the balcony was already filled; the lower level was filled up. Once seating was alright for us, my mother got some popcorn. It was really cool since the popcorn was in a box like in the 1970s and 1980s. The popcorn was also delicious. After we got popcorn, we sat and waited for the movie to begin. When all the previews were finished, the director of the program that allowed *Ponyo* to be shown at Symphony Space came out. He had a few words to say about the movie, then he proceeded to throw out *Ponyo* stuffed dolls and t-shirts. Unfortunately, I was unable to get one for my mother. When the director of the program finished speaking and throwing out souvenirs, the movie began.

After the movie was over at around 5 PM, my mother and I went to Borders. Like I mentioned earlier, at Borders, I was able to get five books. I was really happy about re-upping on books for the rest of the summer. I certainly think the books will be very good. Yesterday was another great day out with my lovely mother.

The Beat, "I Confess," Up-Tempo Ska-Pop Classic: Lyrics, Drums, and Horns Collide For Dope Song

August 6, 2010 (age 14)

The Beat (AKA The English Beat) is certainly one of my favorite bands. Pop and I have all of their albums on vinyl and a greatest hits album CD that we always listen to in the car. It's really hard to maneuver through the CD, though, because we like every song. We both have many favorites; "Mirror in the Bathroom," "Twist & Crawl," "Save It For Later," "Too Nice To Talk To," and many others. But, my favorite song by The Beat is "I Confess."

"I Confess" starts off with a high-pitched piano riff. Then slow tempo rhythmic drums come into the picture, along with some vocals. For the chorus, the song goes into an up-tempo relaxed mode. Horns are coming in and out, and the bass guitar stays strong in the backdrop. The drums are moving all around, and the song has a nice swing to it. Another highlight of the song, is the vocals.

Dave Wakeling's (lead singer) vocals in all of The Beat's songs are energetic. In almost every song, he has a touch that makes you think about any and everything when listening. On "I Confess," his tone is up-tempo and almost sad. He's singing about how he ruined a "two lives," and how he didn't care until he realized that he ruined his as well. That theme and the lyrics are incredibly cool.

The Beat had three albums together, and a number of singles. Most of those singles made their way onto the Beat's best hits album CD that Pop and I have. Since the first time I heard The Beat, I liked their sound and the unity in the songs. The Beat is certainly a group to be studied because of their music. In those three albums, The Beat illustrated ska, jazz, reggae, soul, and pop effortlessly. Unfortunately,

The Beat broke up in 1983, after their final album, *Special Beat Service*. But even though The Beat broke up in 1983, they are one of my favorite groups, and the songs they made together are timeless.

The Yankees Smack the Red Sox, 20-11 to Begin Final Series of the Year

August 22, 2009 (age 13)

The Yankees smacked the Red Sox last night, 20-11. The Red Sox were losing since the first inning and tried their hardest to catch up. However, Yankee hitting would not stop. Every Yankee player scored one run or more, except for Johnny Damon, he got hurt in the first inning. Hideki Matsui had a big impact on the game, with 7 RBI's and two three-run home-runs.

Pitching wasn't on for either team, this was mainly an offensive game. Andy Pettitte gave up 7 runs to the Red Sox. After Pettitte, Brian Bruney and Damaso Marte combined to pitch shutout innings in the 6th and 7th. Then Sergio Mitre came into the game in the 8th, and pitched another shutout inning, then kindly proceeded to give up four runs in the 9th. There goes the 11 runs for the Red Sox.

Red Sox pitching was absolutely horrible, 20 runs is way too much. It all started with Brad Penny, who gave up 8 runs in four innings! Then, Michael Bowden came in the game in the 5th, and gave up a three-run home-run to Matsui. After Matsui, Bowden gave up three more runs in the same inning. The following inning Bowden gave up three more runs. In the 7th, Bowden was taken out and Manny Declarmen was put in. Declarmen gave up one run and was taken out the following inning. After Declarmen, Takashi Saito came in the game, he pitched a shutout inning. However, Saito was taken out for Ramon Ramirez in the 9th inning. In the 9th, Ramirez gave up four more runs; three runs came off the bat of Matsui. Another run came in off of a Swisher double. So there's your ball game, 20-11, Yankees.

Last night was a good game to watch if you wanted to learn how to hit. Since both teams continued to score. However, the Yankees just scored more. The Yankees now have a 7 and a half game lead on the Red Sox. That is a substantial lead heading into the final month of the baseball season before the playoffs.

Reading *The Maltese Falcon*; Big Fan of Mystery Novels and P.I. Books

February 25, 2011 (age 14)

I have a strong, deeply rooted interest in mystery novels and films. *The Maltese Falcon* is on tap for me to read this week, and I can't wait to finish. The story follows a Private eye, Sam Spade, and his partner Miles Archer, who are hired into service by a woman who calls herself Miss Wonderly to follow a man, Floyd Thursby. Wouldn't want to spoil the twist... As a matter of fact, you don't want me to delve into the story too much. That's just enough. This mystery novel, and later film, has enough material to get you through the night.

I've gotten through 50 pages and six chapters of *The Maltese Falcon.* If I made the decision to fully commit to reading the book in a day, I could do it. The writing within keeps me around reading the book. But also the looming film adaptation that has been talked about. I like to be able to compare the book to the film. Both will have separate, quality differences. The only thing I wonder is what will be lost or gained when the novel is made into a film.

The Maltese Falcon set off the Private Investigator genre. Dashiell Hammett practically created the genre. The P.I. themed stories, books, and films then went on to catch fire throughout the film noir period of film. Around the same time, in, around and after, P.I. themed books had an explosion as well. Needless to say, *The Maltese Falcon* would become one of the best P.I. books ever written. There's no doubting the book's significance. Which is why I have more respect, and interest for the genre and book. But the 1930s were a literary force to be reckoned with.

I haven't explored the level of writing in the 1930s yet.

But I'd have to say that *The Maltese Falcon* has me interested in seeing what's to be found in that era. There's a sinister mystery side to all the writings introduced in the time period. The root of all those sinister mysteries must have had something to do with the economy and attitude of the people at the time. Because I think that atmosphere and attitude was captured well in *The Maltese Falcon.*

Economy Has Yet To Hit Movie Pockets

November 10, 2010 (age 14)

After casually looking at box office totals for the majority of the year, I've realized that the economy hasn't hit the movies. As a matter of fact, I don't even have to look at any box office numbers this year to come to that conclusion. All I need to do is look at last year's box office hit, *Avatar*. Let's not forget the significance of that film's success. *Avatar* totaled $749,766,139 at the domestic box office. But this year has also had a huge turnout in the debut weekends for the most popular films.

Throughout this whole economic turmoil, people have certainly gone to the movies frequently. Like I stated before, I'm not surprised. In fact, I think it's been expected that films would continue to do well. Films help give people an outlet from their everyday lives. That's one big reason I want to make films. Some people also look up to actors in films. I've also noticed that those who go and see films can come home with a new perspective on life. I think films are very useful during these times because they can help get people through whatever problems they may be facing. Which is why, I think films continued to do well during the economic struggles.

I think films will continue to do well as the economy slowly returns back to good standing. When that happens, films may have an absolute surge at the box office. I think you could certainly expect lots of money being made over the next three years. But that's not all. As people get back on their feet, the whole atmosphere of the country will change, hopefully for the better, and I think movies will be at the forefront. Nonetheless, as the economy gets better, I think the film industry will be along for that trip.

Thanks to films like *Megamind* and other upcoming films, the table is set for a very prosperous holiday season. This season there are a couple films I'd like to see. For example, *The Tourist*, starring Johnny Depp and Angelina Jolie. I also want to see the latest installment of the *Chronicles of Narnia.* But above all, I can't wait to see *Tron: Legacy.* If all these films do well, I think these films could combine for numbers in the area of $200 or $300 million.

It's too late for films to take a hit now, they've made it through the hard part. I think there's a tunnel with success standing at the end, films haven't reached it yet. But, I think they'll be there relatively soon. Even if that doesn't happen soon, it's inevitable.

Tim Tebow Lands in New York: Why Jets General Manager Mike Tannenbaum and Head Coach Rex Ryan Just Signed their Pink Slips

March 28, 2012 (age 16)

Tim Tebow has arrived in New York. The spectacle of Tebowmania has just begun. As the newest member of the New York Jets football team, the 2nd string quarterback held a press conference two days ago. That unprecedented event drew a crowd of media so large that they took up more space than the Jets regular press area. Just a little hint at what's to come this season. Now that Tebow's here, what's next? What will the Jets and Tim Tebow do on the field? Well that's up in the air right now, who knows how the season will go. But I believe this acquisition will mark the end of the Rex Ryan era.

Mike Tannebaum and Rex Ryan are human. They want to keep their jobs. I understand that. But what I can't understand is who advised the two that this move would result in anything but a catastrophe? Ryan has said plenty times that Mark Sanchez is his quarterback. If that's true, why bring in Tim Tebow? "Your quarterback's" role has just been diminish a great deal by this move, Rex.

If Rex Ryan is serious about his desire to use the wildcat formation more, that's more time taken away from Mark Sanchez under center. Is this the Playoffs plan that Rex Ryan envisions? If so, I don't see it working for various reasons.

When Mark Sanchez throws two incompletions, and the Jets go three and out, what will the fans chant? Last year, all the fans could do was boo. This year, they can scream at the top of their lungs for Tim Tebow. Big problem. What about the locker room? When Sanchez falls into a little slump and Tebow succeeds for a game, who will the players go to now? The locker room would be split in half. And if you thought last year was bad? This year may be even worse. The team's morale will just be shot and everybody will be on edge. But putting the locker room turmoil aside for a moment, how will the Jets even run a successful offense with Tim Tebow?

From Tebow's mechanics, to his poor decision-making skills, the game could just slip away. Tebow is listed as a quarterback, but most of the time, he plays like a converted running back that played quarterback in high school. Everybody in the NFL knows he's not your prototypical pocket passer, something that the Jets need to win, something that they already have. The Jets offense wasn't built around a scrambling quarterback and weak mechanics. The offense was built around a solid pocket passer. Who knows what's gonna happen now.

The Jets already had a tough road ahead of them this season. Their cross-town rival just won the Super Bowl, they have plenty of holes to fill on both sides of the ball, and they had chemistry problems. Now that Tim Tebow has arrived, that road has gotten a lot tougher. Tim Tebow is a distraction. Don't get me wrong, I respect him for what he does, and the person that he is. But I don't think he'll benefit the Jets by being on their roster every Sunday. I don't see Tim Tebow and the Jets succeeding, when he's under center, or even two feet behind. The Jets team that you see right now, may never recover from this bad decision, and the front office will take a hit as well.

Editor's note: Mike Tannebaum is no longer the General Manager of The Jets. He was fired after the 2012 season. Rex Ryan remains the Head Coach. At the time of this publishing, Tim Tebow is still member of the Jets football team.

Summer Film Camp Over: Thank You, NYFA!

August 3, 2009 (age 13)

Friday was the last day at film camp this summer for me. Camp was only two weeks, but it felt much longer, and that's a good thing. Film camp was a lot of fun, and I met a lot of new people. Plus, I learned even more this session compared to the Winter session at NYFA. For Winter session, I was at Union Square, and during the Summer session, I was at Millenium High School.

Film camp was a lot of fun. We did so much hands-on activities in camp. However, we were working with different cameras from before. The cameras we used during camp were nowhere near as good as the cameras from my Winter session. But we were able to make do with what we had. During camp, I even got to go to Battery Park for the first time. We went there for a camera test, similar to the camera tests I did in the Winter session. I went to Battery park twice since one of my friends shot his movie there.

In camp I met a lot of people. Some I met on the first day of camp. But most, I met as time went along. I was really cool with five people. However, I was cool with every one in the camp. Martin, Avery, J.T., Dean, and Sumir were like my best friends in camp. Usually, we were all in different groups, but when we had lunch and breaks, we would talk about a number of things. We all had the same interests. Then there were the TA's (Teaching Assistants). We automatically hit it off, I think we got along because I was one of the oldest in the class, and because I'd already shot my own film before. Gabe, Naren, and Dave were the main TA's I was cool with.

The second week of Summer film camp included all of the remaining children filming their movies. I shot my movie, *The Day Dreamer* on Wednesday. *The Day Dreamer* is about a Teenage day trader who day dreams. The shoot went well and I had three days to edit. When it came time to edit, I learned a lot that I didn't know about final cut pro. The TA's knew a great deal about the software, they were able to help me a lot. Editing certainly went well.

The screening for all the films was last Friday. Most of the films looked good. I like how all the films came out. I liked how my film came out, except for one part. This film camp was great and even better than my last session. Thank You, NYFA.

Afterword

When I was 13 years old, I promised myself that I would write and publish my first book at 16. At the time, I had written my first complete short story. It wasn't really that good, but I liked the characters I created. Around the same time, I started writing film and literary criticsm.

One day, after I finished writing a film review, my father gave me a poetry prompt. I didn't see this coming, and I didn't really know what to think or what to write about. Poetry? I thought. Why is Pop making me write poetry? But after a couple laughs, I dove right into it. Seeing as how it was my first poem, I didn't think it would be all that great. But my father was ecstatic! He had to leave the room to collect his thoughts. When he returned, he had a new plan for me. He told me from now own, I had to write three poems a day. So, that's what did.

Writing poetry was cultivating a skill I didn't know I had, and it was helping me to improve my other writing. Looking back, I don't know how I found the time for it, but I did. And in hindsight, I'm glad now because at the time, I didn't know I would use some of my poems in my first book.

Well, all things told, I'm happy to say that at 16, I'm humbled by the thought of writing and publishing my first book. Reflecting on my work brings me great joy, and it has certainly inspired and motivated me to write more books, something I've always wanted to do. I also hope that this book will put me in a position to help other teens write and publish their books, something else I've always wanted to do. Finally, I hope that readers of all ages, but especially other teenagers, will appreciate and enjoy *Performance Day.*

—Amir Ali Said, 2012, Brooklyn, NY

ABOUT THE AUTHOR

Amir Ali Said is a writer, actor, and director, and avid sports fan from Brooklyn, NY. At just 16 years old, he has amassed an impressive list of credits. With feature roles in films and television shows such as *Inside Man*; *Game 6*; *Be Kind Rewind; Law & Order: Criminal Intent*, and more, Amir has successfully demonstrated his broad acting range—appearing equally comfortable in both dramatic and comedic roles. A writer since the age of 5, Amir has written a number of short stories, poems, editorials, and more. In 2008, he wrote and directed his first short film, *The Fart Police*; and in 2009, he wrote and directed his second short film, *The Daydreamer*. Both of Amir's short films were featured in New York Film Academy's Tweens Film Showcase (2008, 2009, respectively). In 2011, Amir wrote and starred in his first play, *I See Things in Scenes*; and in 2012, Amir wrote and helped produced his second play, *The Affair of Agnes Miller*, based on his short story of the same name. Both of his plays were featured in the Writopia Bestival.

www.ingramcontent.com/pod-product-compliance
Lightning Source LLC
Chambersburg PA
CBHW050313110726
47899CB00007B/2222

* 9 7 8 0 9 7 4 9 7 0 4 4 8 *